Dina Ba...

A New
Way

CHIARA LUBICH

A New Way

The Spirituality of Unity

Published in the United States by New City Press
202 Cardinal Rd., Hyde Park, NY 12538
www.newcitypress.com
©2006 New City Press (English translation)

Translated by the New City editorial staff
from the original Italian *Una via nuova*
©2002 Città Nuova Editrice, Rome, Italy

Cover design by Durva Correia

Library of Congress Cataloging-in-Publication Data:

Lubich, Chiara, 1920-

  [Via nuova. English]
  A new way : the spirituality of unity / Chiara Lubich ; [translated by the New City editorial staff].
     p. cm.
  ISBN-13: 978-1-56548-236-4 (alk. paper)
  ISBN-10: 1-56548-236-0 (alk. paper)
  1. Spirituality--Catholic Church. 2. Catholic Church--Doctrines I. Title
  BX2350.65.L8413 2006
  248.4'82-dc22

Printed in the United States of America

Contents

Preface

As I meditate upon this book by Chiara Lubich, in my heart emerges the same faith-based conviction seen in Scripture: "The spirit of the Lord fills the whole world, and that which holds everything together knows all that is said" (Wis 1:7).

Often, nowadays, the shadows that thicken around the human race trouble or almost overwhelm us. But when we let the Holy Spirit illuminate our hearts and open up our eyes, we are flooded with hope and joy. The Spirit is God's power at work. And we, reading the signs of the times (cf. Mt 16:3), are able to discern the Spirit's active presence all over the world. As John Paul II reminded us as the third millennium approached: "There is also need for a better appreciation and under-standing of the signs of hope present in the last part of this century" (*Tertio Millennio Adveniente*, 46).

The Spirit has been manifested with particular vigor in certain aspects of the Church's life. In the last few decades, in many different ways, the Spirit has been bringing about renewal within the Church. I am thinking here particularly of his powerful action during the Second Vatican Council. And I am thinking also of those practical examples of new life inspired by the Spirit in the form of the modern ecclesial Movements, those that arose before as well as those that arose after the watershed moment of Vatican II. They represent not only sure signs of the new springtime of the Church foreseen by recent Popes, but also the "medicine" that everyone knows will cure the ills of today's world. It was not by chance, therefore, that John Paul II invited us to "a renewed appreciation of the presence and activity of the Spirit, who acts within the Church" (ibid. 45).

This book provides an attractive witness to this hopeful attitude. Meditating upon the richness of its pages, the mind turns spontaneously to that passage in the Gospel of John in which Jesus promises his Comforting Spirit who will guide the People of God "into all truth" (cf. 16:13), unfolding the Gospel of Christ through time and in space.

Although a host of profoundly dramatic contradictions have marked the entire twentieth century, it was rich with currents of renewal. The action of the Spirit, beginning with the biblical, patristic and liturgical movements that prepared the way for Vatican II, pervaded it. These brought Christianity back into touch with its origins, making it rediscover the initial intensity and genuineness of life in the early Church. Among these revitalizing forces we should also recall the encyclical *Mystici Corporis* (1943), in which Pope Pius XII held up before the entire People of God its own nature as communion among brothers and sisters who have Christ as their head.

It is a significant coincidence that in the very same year, as the bombs of the Second World War fell on the city of Trent in Northern Italy, the "charism of unity" first appeared. The charism led Chiara Lubich and her original group of companions to take "a solemn shift towards other people," making them become, without reservation, servants of all their neighbors and inspiring

8

them to explore the great art of "becoming saints together." Twenty years before Vatican II a spiritual pathway that corresponded providentially to its call for a new style of Church life had come into being, one that would help the Church proceed with enthusiasm to take the living Jesus to everyone in today's world.

The charism of the Movement, those of other ecclesial Movements, and the renewal brought about by Vatican II manifest that long before any talk of "globalization" the Spirit had already begun to give rise in human hearts to his more true alternative: the globalization of love. The idea of universal "brotherhood" requires us to see all men and women first of all as children of the same Father and therefore all worthy of the same love. Only a love like this, which reaches out to the whole world — as is clearly underlined and promoted by the spirituality of unity put forward in this book — can offer new and life-giving energy to modern culture. Beginning with the French Revolution, the process of secularizing modern culture has led Western society up a blind alley by gradually diminishing its capacity to safeguard the dignity of the human person.

I am sure that the life of the Risen Lord present among people united in love for one another — that "something more" which the spirituality of unity demands in contrast to other spiritual ways with their more "individual" lifestyle — will provide an effective source of renewal in the Church. Moreover, it offers a remedy that can heal the crises of today's world, caused for the most part by various forms of disunity and division.

In fact, Vatican II presented with great clarity the Church as *a sign and instrument of the unity of the whole human race* (cf. *Lumen Gentium*, 1). Rooting itself firmly in the life of the three divine Persons (cf. ibid. 4), the People of God is called to model the unity of the whole human community. Its primary service to the human family must be to bring the world to experience communion. As John Paul II wrote: "To make the Church *the home and the school of communion*: that is the great challenge facing us in the millennium which is now beginning, if we wish to be faithful to God's plan and respond to the world's deepest yearnings" (*Novo Millennio Ineunte*, 43).

The spirituality of communion that John Paul II recommended to the whole Church on the threshold of the new millennium is not merely one variant of the Church's life. It is an absolute necessity, the indispensable instrument for the Church to fulfill its true reason for being on earth.

Therefore, Christians have the urgent obligation to create living cells of the Church as communion everywhere. At the same time, this is the starting point of the new evangelization: we must begin by evangelizing ourselves completely, and to be evangelized we must enter always more fully into the Trinity's way of being — that is, into communion.

All the key points of classic Christian spirituality offer fundamental guidelines for progressing on the spiritual journey, but this book brings to light their distinctly communitarian dimension — beginning with God who is love and proceeding to doing the will of God, to Mary and to the Holy Spirit. However, the newest and most original feature of the vision of the Christian mystery outlined here is the dual reality of *unity and Jesus Forsaken*, understood as the two sides of the same coin.

Knowing how to embrace Jesus Forsaken is the necessary condition "to 'make room' for our brothers and sisters, bearing 'each other's burdens' (Gal 6:2) and resisting the selfish temptations which constantly beset us" (ibid). This attitude, if it becomes mutual, generates the presence of Jesus in the midst, a true exterior castle (cf. the end of chapter 1 of the present volume). This exterior castle, on a par with and complementary to the "interior" castle that Teresa of Avila speaks about, cannot remain a perquisite solely of the Focolare Movement. It is a vitally important source of strength and life for the body of the Church, as well for the whole social body.

The spirituality of communion, also called a "collective" spirituality because it brings people to be "one" in Christ (cf. Gal 3), makes it clear to Christians that the time is ripe to direct our energies beyond the Church. Following the way of communion and of unity, we live the full meaning of our baptism: we are grafted into the life of the Father, the Son and the Holy Spirit, and we become faithful adults, able to expand the Trinitarian life of the Church into society.

Could we expect any less from a genuine Christian life? By living the spirituality of communion we avoid the danger of extremism, both that of conforming to the one-dimensional earth-boundness of so much of today's culture and that of retreating into a sterile spiritualism. "Lending God our humanity" we have the possibility of bringing to life a holiness of the people and flooding the world with the divine, incarnating in daily life the love that *uplifts*, that *heals*, that *creates a home* and so on, with all the good effects that flow from this to the Church and to human society in general.

Bit by bit, from a small seed, projects that have immense repercussions come to life.

The love that is *communion* has given rise in the last few years to hundreds of businesses that follow the principles of an economy of communion — an original paradigm for industry that is stirring up growing interest even among economists.

The love that *radiates* has led so far to the construction of about twenty-five "Permanent Mariapolises" — small, modern settlements that, like the city set on a hill, give witness to the possibility of a society governed by the law of gospel love.

The love that *creates a home*, in the widest sense of the word, demonstrates through new expressions of artistic inspiration that in addition to being the Good and the True, God is also Beauty.

The love that *generates wisdom* helps to elaborate the intellectual understanding implicit in the charism of unity, re-examining in its light theology, philosophy, psychology, and all the various sciences to the point of opening up, in this post-modern age that tends to see reality in fragmented ways, a new synthesis of human knowledge.

Love, "the spark that inspires everything done under the name of Focolare" (John Paul II), has all these effects, and much more, wherever this spirituality and life of communion has reached in the world.

Consequently, this book puts us in touch with the great "projects" of the Holy Spirit for the renewal of the world — projects that open up horizons beyond all human expectation, yet which nonetheless already show concrete results. It gives rise to profound gratitude and great joy in those who have had the grace to meet and follow the spirituality of unity, however they do so. Where it is at work the presence of God who is near (the Immanuel, God-with-us) and the action of the Holy Spirit are obvious in the Church and in today's society. We must thank the Father for this gift that we are witnessing at the beginning of the third millennium.

What, therefore, do I wish for this book? That it may become nourishment for the lives of many and that it may contribute to making the Church beautiful, so that for the salvation of the world and for the glory of God the Church may live among men and women, as a sign of and a pointer towards happiness.

May Mary, whose womb generated the source of this spirituality of unity and from whom the Movement takes its name as the Work of Mary, be for all of us *Hodigitria*, that is, the one who points out the way.

Miloslav Cardinal Vlk
Archbishop of Prague

Part 1

Basic Structure

A New Spirituality
that is Communitarian

In this chapter we should like to begin by focusing on the spiritual aspect of the Focolare Movement[1] and in particular on what is unique and characteristic in its spirituality: its being communitarian or, better, "collective," as Paul VI called it.

The Beauty of the Spiritualities

We know that in these two thousand years since the coming of Jesus, all the churches — insofar as they were faithful to the Word of the Lord and to the inspiration of the Holy Spirit — have seen a flowering of spiritualities in their wombs. One after another and sometimes all together, the most beautiful, the most profound, the richest experiences of spiritual life have been born, so that the Bride of Christ is adorned with pearls most precious and diamonds most rare that have formed and will continue to form many saints.

Thus, as we have often said, if Jesus is the Word made flesh, the Church — in the abundance of all its spiritual

---

1. Please note that throughout this publication the names Focolare Movement, Focolare, and Work of Mary will be used interchangeably.

experiences down through the centuries — appears like the Gospel unfolded in time and space.

Going to God Individually

In all these splendid spiritualities, one note always remains constant: it is, above all, the individual person alone who goes to God.

Various studies and the relevant research of our scholars show (at least in a general sense) that a spirituality of unity like that of the Focolare, with its particular emphasis on the communitarian aspects of the Christian life, is now appearing in the Church for the first time.

They say that specific experiences in the past have come close to it, especially those in which love was at the basis of the spiritual life. Here we recall Basil, who placed the first commandment regarding love of God and the second regarding love of neighbor at the basis of the life of his community. And, above all, Augustine comes to mind. For him, mutual love and unity were of supreme value. This is why we feel particularly close to him.

However, Father Jesus Castellano, a renowned scholar in the field of spiritual theology, says that

> In the history of Christian spirituality we hear, "Christ is in me; he lives within me," which is the perspective of the individual spirituality, of life in Christ, or we hear, "Christ is present in our brothers and sisters," which is the perspective of charity, of the works of charity. But the decisive further step is

missing, that is, to discover that if Christ is in me as he is also in the other person, then Christ in me loves Christ in you and vice versa . . . there is giving and receiving.[2]

I would add here that many great founders do call for mutual love in their various rules.[3]

Going to God Together

Father Castellano continues:

There is also a communitarian spirituality, ecclesial, modelled on the Mystical Body. . . . This spirituality is usually referred to as being characteristic of the present day, a current of spirituality of our century, the century of the rediscovery of the Church. But the "something more" that the Focolare offers with its collective spirituality is the vision and practice of a communion, of an ecclesial life, modelled on the Mystical Body, in which there exists the personal gift of each to the other and the dimension of becoming "one." Even when in present-day authors there are intuitions or statements concerning this dimension of theology and spirituality, they lack any suggestion of how, practically, to turn it into a lifestyle, and incarnate it in an experience, such as that lived by the Focolare Movement: from the simplest things,

2. Jesus Castellano, O.C.D., Letter to Chiara Lubich (regarding the Focolare's collective spirituality of unity), 21 June 1992.
3. See pp. 49 to 50.

such as "keeping Jesus in our midst,"[4] which is the Movement's *alpha* and its *omega*, to its more demanding dimensions.

In the history of spirituality there are a few examples of experiences in collective spirituality, in reciprocal giving — just a few, to tell the truth. . . . But even these rare experiences were not offered as a teaching and, much less, as a spirituality to be lived daily, within the reach of everyone.

Certainly, spirituality centered on the in-dwelling of the Trinity exists, but at an individual level. Normally, its authors do not connect this indwelling with the awareness of a communion between persons who have the same grace. . . . They do not reach the point of saying, as is the case in the Focolare, "If the Trinity is in me and in you, then the Trinity is among us, we are in a Trinitarian relationship. . . . Therefore our relationship is in the image of the Trinity; indeed, it is the Trinity that lives this relationship in us."[5]

Up to this point, then, we have listened to Father Castellano.

---

4. This expression refers to the commitment, taken by those who live the spirituality of unity, to fulfill the new commandment of Jesus so that his promise may come true, "For where two or three are gathered in my name, I am there among them" (Mt 18:20). See also pp. 34 to 35.
5. Letter to Chiara Lubich, 21 June 1992.

Our Times Demand It

Other modern theologians have foreseen a collective spirituality for our times, and the Second Vatican Council called for one.

In speaking of the Church's spirituality of the future, Karl Rahner imagines it as being in a "fraternal communion in which it is possible to make the same basic experience of the Spirit together." He says:

> Those of us who are older . . . have been spiritually formed in an individualist way. . . . If there ever was an experience of the Spirit that took place among people as a group and normally understood as such, . . . it is the experience of the first Pentecost in the Church, an event — we must presume — that certainly did not consist in the casual meeting of a collection of mystics who lived individually, but in the experience of the Spirit had by the community. . . . I think that in a future spirituality the element of fraternal spiritual communion, of a spirituality lived together, would play a more decisive role, and that slowly but surely we must go in this direction.[6]

Directing its attention to the Church as the body of Christ and as a people gathered in the Trinitarian bond of love, the Second Vatican Council "modifies," writes De Fiores, "the underlying framework of spiritual life and pastoral care, giving it a more ecclesial meaning.

---

6. Karl Rahner, "Elementi di spiritualità nella Chiesa del futuro," in *Problemi e prospettive di spiritualità*, edited by T. Goffi and B. Secondin (Brescia, 1983), pp. 440–441.

The salvation and perfection of one's own soul, about which preachers and spiritual authors insisted, is freed from an individualistic preoccupation. . . . One feels the need . . . to live intensely the bonds of a brotherhood based on the Gospel to the point of forming a community like that of the early Christians, described in an ideal way in the Acts of the Apostles."[7]

When he was still a cardinal, Pope Paul VI said that what once had been an isolated experience must in our times become habitual, and that the exceptional figure of the saint, although venerated, must give way, in a certain sense, to the sanctity of the people, that is, to the people of God who become saints.[8]

We are living in an age when the life of communion comes fully into light. Besides seeking the reign of God in individual souls, we seek the reign of God in the midst of souls.

Early Indications of a Collective Spirituality

But how can we describe our communitarian spirituality? What are its characteristics?

First of all, let us see how it came about, and if there are significant events that were indicative of what was to come.

One early sign could be that longing we expressed as the war raged around us: if we were to die, our common desire was to be buried in only one tomb with these words written on it: "And we have believed in love."

7. S. De Fiores, "Spiritualità contemporanea," in *Nuovo dizionario di spiritualità* (Rome, 1978), p. 1535.
8. Cf. G. B. Cardinal Montini, *Discorsi su la Madonna e su i Santi (1955–1962)* (Milan, 1965), pp. 499–500.

It was this faith in love that made us begin our new way of life by loving the poor in the widest variety of ways.[9] This experience soon made us understand that in order to be Christians we had to love each and every neighbor.

And from this starting point in which all of us in the initial group of Focolarine[10] began to love every neighbor, there came about the practical realization of the new commandment, and a decisive commitment by each of us that was formulated in a kind of pact: "I am ready to die for you; and I for you; all of us for each one of us."

In later years, this pact was recognized as the foundation upon which all of the Focolare Movement was

---

9. "We read: 'Just as you did to one of the least of these who are members of my family, you did it to me' (cf. Mt 25:40). The people around us, due to the terrible circumstances, were hungry, thirsty, and wounded. They were without food and shelter. We used to cook large kettles of soup which we distributed to them. Sometimes the poor knocked on the door of our house, and we invited them to sit down interspersed among us, one of the poor and one of us, and then another of the poor and one of us.

"The gospel assures: 'Ask, and it will be given to you' (Mt 7:7; Lk 11:9). We asked for the poor and every time we were filled with all kinds of goods from God: bread, powdered milk, jam, wood, clothing . . . all of which we took to those who were in need of these things.

"One day a poor person asked for a pair of shoes size 42 [European continent measure]. One of us addressed this prayer before the tabernacle in church: 'Give me, Lord, a pair of shoes size 42 for you in that poor person.'

"On leaving the church a young lady, a friend of hers, presented her with a package. She opened it and there was a pair of shoes size 42. And this is only one of thousands upon thousands of examples" (Chiara Lubich, *La dottrina spirituale* [Milan: Arnaldo Mondadori Editore, 2001] p. 46).

10. The original Italian terms are used throughout this book to indicate those members of the Focolare Movement who live in community: Focolari*na*: a member of a women's focolare house; plural: Focolari*ne*. Focolari*no*: a member of a men's focolare house; plural: Focolari*ni* (also used to indicate men and women collectively).

built. This pact revealed what the nature of the Movement had to be: mutual love that gives rise to a collective spirituality.

That was the key event of those first days of our life, which required, as a consequence, the sharing of our experiences and the communion of goods.

This mutual love had to reach the point of our being consumed in one, of making us experience unity.

Then there was the time in the cellar when we read Jesus' testament,[11] which appeared to us as the "founding charter" of what was coming to life.

We practiced such a radical and total love for our neighbor that it made us cease to have any other objective, even that of sanctity as it was understood at that time. If we, called to a new way, had followed the idea of sanctity as it was understood then, it would have been tarnished with self-love or egoism. For us, personal sanctity would result instead from our living unity.

Then we had our initial ideas about fraternal unity. In 1947, after we had experienced it, we gave unity the following definition:

---

11. "It was 1943. The war was also breaking out in Trent. Ruins, rubble, death.

"For various reasons I got to know several young people of about my own age.

"One day I found myself together with my new companions in a dark cellar, with a lighted candle and the New Testament in my hands. I opened it. There was Jesus' prayer before dying: 'Father . . . may they all be one' (Jn 17:11, 21). It was not an easy text to understand given our education, but those words seemed to be luminously clear; one by one they put in our hearts the conviction that we were born for that page of the gospel" (Chiara Lubich, *La dottrina spirituale*, p. 44).

"Oh! Unity, unity! What divine beauty! We do not have human words to express it! It is Jesus!"

The Needs of the Past

In past centuries, the idea of going to God alone was common. This was a consequence of circumstances dating back to that distant period in history in which the fervor of the early Christians, which had witnessed the community of Jerusalem coming together in one heart and one soul, had begun to grow less. The period of persecutions had come to an end, and many decided to save their faith by withdrawing to the desert. It was the age of hermits.

While this preserved many Christian principles and helped a number of the hermits become saints, often the importance of other people was undervalued. They were even seen as an obstacle on the way to God.

Abba Arsenius said, "Flee from human beings, and you will be saved,"[12] and, "I cannot be simultaneously with God and with human beings."[13]

Many centuries later we still find similar teachings. In the famous book, *The Imitation of Christ*, we read:

> The most holy men and women who ever lived fled, as far as they could, from human company, and chose to serve God in the secret of their hearts. One holy man said: "Each time I have been in the company of people, I have come away less of a person myself. . . ." Therefore, our Lord and his angels will

---

12. L. Mortari (ed.), *Vita e detti dei Padri del deserto* (Rome, 1975), p. 97.
13. Mortari, *Vita e detti dei Padri del deserto*, pp. 99–100.

draw near and abide with those who withdraw from their acquaintances and their friends.[14]

They were "individual" spiritualities, therefore, even though, because of the mystery of the Mystical Body, they were never exclusively individual insofar as what happens to one person always has a reflection upon others. And also because these Christians offered to God long prayers and heavy penances on behalf of their brothers and sisters.

The Needs of the Present Time

But times have changed.

The Holy Spirit is now forcefully calling men and women to walk side by side with other people, indeed, to be one heart and one soul with all those who so desire.

Twenty years before the Council, the Holy Spirit impelled our Movement to make this solemn change of direction toward others. In the spirituality of unity, we go to God through our neighbor. "I – my neighbor – God," we used to say. We go to God together with humanity, together with our brothers and sisters; even more so, we go to God *by way of* human beings.

Characteristic Features of Individual Spiritualities

But what is the difference between an individual spirituality and a communitarian or collective spirituality?

---

14. *The Imitation of Christ* I, XX, 1–6.

An individual spirituality usually has specific requirements:

— Solitude and fleeing from people are needed in order to reach mystical union with the Trinity within one's self. A typical example is the way of Teresa of Avila, who sought to be united to the Lord in his dwelling-place at the center of her heart.

— In order to safeguard solitude, silence is necessary.

— In order to keep far from people, veils are worn and the enclosed life of the cloister is sought, in addition to wearing a special habit.

— In order to imitate the passion of Christ, the most varied and at times rigorous penances, fasting and vigils are undertaken.

— There is submission in obedience to a superior.

— There are also the vows of chastity and poverty.

— Some withdraw into their cells for long periods of time to pray and to meditate.

Tools or Instruments of a Collective Spirituality

ONE'S NEIGHBOR

In our collective way, we too look for solitude and silence. We do so in order to listen well to the voice of God in our hearts: to live out Jesus' invitation to pray behind closed doors, and to plunge into the depths of union with God, as he did himself on the mountain; to avoid useless words . . . and to escape other people if they lead us to sin. But usually we welcome our brothers and sisters; we love Christ in our neighbor, in every neighbor — Christ who can be alive or can be reborn in our neighbor also through our help. We wish to be united with others in the name of Jesus, so as to be sure of his presence among us (cf. Mt 18:20).

In the individual spiritualities it is as if we were standing in a magnificent garden (the Church) observing and admiring only one flower: the presence of God within oneself. In a collective spirituality, we love and admire all the flowers of the garden, every presence of Christ in other persons. And we love his presence in others as we do in ourselves.

And since our way is not, nor could it ever be, only communitarian, but is also fully personal (we must remember that we will be on our own when we present ourselves to God for judgment), most of us have the experience that when we are alone, after having loved our neighbors, we are aware in our souls of union with God. Indeed it is enough, for instance, just to pick up a book for meditation to find that God wants to begin a conversation with us.

In this light, then, we can say that those who approach their neighbors in the correct way, that is, according to the gospel, loving as the gospel teaches, find that they become more Christ, more fully human.

THE WORD

Since we seek to be united with our brothers and sisters, we love the word, which is a means of communication.

In the Movement we use the words to "make ourselves one"[15] with our neighbors with the "technique of

---

15. This is the attitude that Paul speaks about. It implies sharing with others in the conditions of their lives, in their joys or pains, tastes, mentality, etc. "I made myself weak with the weak, I made myself all things to all . . ." (1 Cor 9:22) (see also p. 44).

unity,"[16] to the point that the other person or persons, fully convinced that they are loved, find the courage to love in return, and they too become part of this collective way.

The word is used by those in positions of responsibility when they speak "one to one" with others, to help them persevere on the way of perfection (if we do not go ahead, we go backward). They illuminate, give advice, instruct, always waiting in total self-emptiness for the Holy Spirit to suggest the right word for that particular person at that moment.

We use the word in our various communities when we tell one another our experiences about putting into practice the Word of Life[17] or about our spiritual lives, aware that if fire is not passed on to others, it goes out, and that this communion of soul is of tremendous spiritual value. Saint Lawrence Giustiniani explains this beautifully:

> Nothing in the world renders more praise to God and reveals him worthy of praise more than the humble and fraternal exchange of spiritual gifts; since charity, which cannot exist if people live in solitude, is reinforced by these very same gifts. . . . The Lord . . . has commanded us to exercise this virtue toward our brothers and sisters always, in word and

---

16. A series of principles taken from the New Testament, especially the four gospels and Paul, which the author summarizes thus: "Loving everyone; being the first to love; loving others as ourselves; making ourselves one; loving Jesus in our neighbor." This has come to be termed the "art of loving," but initially, since its aim was to lead people to unity, it was called the "technique of unity."

17. The "Word of Life" (cf. Phil 2:16) is a sentence from scriptures, which members and friends of the Focolare try to understand and live for a specific period of time.

deed. Therefore, if we do not wish to be transgressors of his law and under judgment as persons who carelessly disregard the salvation of our brothers and sisters, all of us who have received graces from heaven should make every effort to share with others the divine gifts we have received, especially the gifts that can help others along the way of perfection.[18]

Furthermore, we use the word during the "moment of truth"[19] when brothers or sisters, through their negative or positive observations, help one another to become saints together.

We use the word during our public meetings of whatever size they may be, in order to keep the fire of love for God ablaze and to achieve the Work of Mary's[20] specific goals.

And when we do not use the word by speaking, we do so by writing: we write letters, articles, books, and diaries so that the kingdom of God may go ahead in many hearts. We use all the modern means of communication.

But whenever we speak or write it should always be a "heavenly speaking," something promoting supernatural life, in accordance with the words of Paul: "You must look for the things that are in heaven; let your thoughts be on heavenly things" (Col 3:1–2). And anything that does not comply with this, should be decisively mortified.

---

18. St. Lawrence Giustiniani, *Disciplina e perfezione della vita monastica* (Rome, 1967), p. 4.
19. This practice derives its origin from the practice of fraternal correction contained in the gospel (cf. Mt 18:15–17).
20. The Work of Mary is the Focolare Movement. It is the name under which the Movement was approved by the Roman Catholic Church.

Penances and Vows at the Service of Unity

In our collective spirituality there are no veils nor grills nor particular religious dress to distinguish us from others (unless this is clearly God's will for us, especially if we are members of a religious order). Generally, so as not to separate ourselves from others, we dress like them, in harmony with our environment, intermingling with everyone, because nothing should prevent our love from reaching each person.

In the Focolare Movement, too, we practice those mortifications that are indispensable for any Christian life. We do penances, especially those recommended by the Church, but we hold the highest regard for those that come from the life of unity with our brothers and sisters. We know that unity is not easy for the old self,[21] as Paul calls it, which always lives within us.

Furthermore, unity is not achieved once and for all; it always has to be re-built. When there is unity, and through it, we have the presence of Jesus in our midst, we experience immense joy, that joy promised by Jesus in his prayer for unity. When unity diminishes, however, nothing makes sense, we lose our bearings. We live in a kind of purgatory. This is the penance we must be ready to face.

What must come into play here is our love for Jesus

---

21. In the Pauline sense of human nature that is a slave to the ego (cf. Eph 4:22).

crucified and forsaken, the key to unity.[22] Out of love for him, first we overcome every suffering within ourselves, and then we make every effort to rebuild unity.

The Holy Spirit taught us quite early on about this penance.

As early as 1945 I wrote: "Do not be afraid to suffer. . . . But seek the suffering that is offered to you by God's will . . . that specific will of God which is mutual love — the new commandment — the pearl of the gospel. . . .

"Then, drawn by the cross . . . you will work to fuse your small community into a single body, and this will give great glory to God! Then God will live among you, and you will feel it. You will rejoice in his presence: he will give you his light, inflame you with his love! But to reach this point, you must vow yourselves completely to Christ crucified."

As far as vows are concerned, there are people in the Work of Mary who take them. For these people, while a vow may have, as it does for everyone, an ascetical purpose (mortification of the self through obedience, of the flesh through chastity, of attachment to material

_____

22. The cry of Jesus crucified: "My God, my God, why have you forsaken me?" (Mk 15:34; Mt 27:46) is at the center of the spirituality of Chiara Lubich. Jesus, the one who experienced the separation between human beings with God and among themselves, and the one who also knew how to overcome this immense test by re-abandoning himself to the Father (cf. Lk 23:46), manifested himself to Chiara as the key to unity. In fact, seeing his countenance in every personal and collective suffering, embracing him wholeheartedly and getting on with doing God's will in the following moment, Chiara Lubich found the way to pass continually from death to life and to accomplish unity everywhere — unity in which the Risen One is present and gives the experience of the fruits of his Spirit (see also pp. 51 to 53).

things through poverty), a vow has a particular meaning from the point of view of our collective spirituality: it also serves decisively as a support for unity, it serves the community. The vow of obedience is made to ensure unity with our superiors; the vow of chastity so as to have a pure heart ready to love Jesus in every neighbor; the vow of poverty so as to be free to put into practice the communion of goods with our brothers or sisters.

Prayer in Common

We also pray in the Movement, and we especially value liturgical prayer, such as the Mass with the most holy Eucharist, because it is the prayer of the Church. We can leave aside everything else if serious obstacles arise, but never the Mass.

Typical of us is prayer together as taught by Jesus, which we call "Consenserint," because it goes back to his words: "If two of you agree [Latin: *consenserint*] on earth about anything you ask, it will be done for you by my Father in heaven" (Mt 18:19).

When we meditate, we base our meditation on sacred scripture or on writings of our own spirituality. Then, at the right moment, we share with our brothers or sisters the fruit of our meditation, since we want to pursue the sanctity of the others as much as our own.

In the Movement we also have days of retreat and spiritual exercises. The program contains spiritual subjects for meditation in silence and solitude, but also talking and the chance to communicate with one another so as to build each other up.

Jesus in Our Midst

In the more individual ways to God, Christians must often follow a certain ascent in loving God; they climb various steps, as they go towards the mountain of perfection.

While the collective way also has the dimension of progress, it tends rather to place the Christian immediately at the peak, on top. This is because of the presence of Jesus in the midst.[23] Jesus, who lives in the midst of us and in each person, cannot be merely half-way: he is always perfect. If there is growth in Jesus, it is a growth in perfection.

In the collective way, being already on top, we walk along the crest of the mountain, overcoming all the big and small trials with Jesus crucified and forsaken, until we reach the goal that God has marked out for us.

For all of us who walk along the way of unity, Jesus in the midst is essential.

On pain of personal failure, we must always revive his presence in all our centers and communities. And if God's will means we have to be far from others and alone, while we are supported by our love for Jesus crucified and forsaken, we must seek every opportunity to establish his presence with a brother or sister of the Ideal.[24] Only in this way will we always have light, strength, peace and enthusiasm.

---

23. See pp. 56 to 61.
24. Ever since the time of the Second World War Chiara Lubich gave the name "Ideal" to that light which they felt had been given to them and which they felt came as inspiration from on high. The term covers all the ideas that are the foundation and the life of the Focolare Movement.

It is Jesus in our midst who brings about the "something more" that is a characteristic of our charism. Just as two electric poles make no light until they are united, but as soon as they are united they do, likewise, two persons do not experience the typical light of this charism until they are united in Christ through love.

Jesus in our midst is the very nature of our life, not just an occasional presence among us. He must always be present. His presence is not only a point of arrival; it is also a point of departure: "Above all, hold unfailing your love for one another" (1 Pt 4:8).

Everything has meaning and value for us if we have Jesus in the midst. This is the "norm of norms,"[25] and it is true of apostolic activities, in our studies, at work, as well as in prayer and in our striving towards holiness.

We will reach sanctity if we march towards God in unity.

The "Exterior" Castle

Teresa of Avila, a doctor of the Church, speaks of an "interior castle," that is, the presence of God's Majesty dwelling in the center of the soul, which is to be discovered and illuminated during the course of life by overcoming various trials. This is a high-point of holiness in

---

25. The author is referring to the highly regarded principle in the Movement of always maintaining mutual love in the first place and in everything. This principle was then adopted as the Premise of the General Statutes of the Work of Mary and the various Regulations of its branches. It is stated in this way: "Mutual and constant love, which makes unity and the presence of Jesus in the community possible, is for the persons who are part of the Work of Mary the basis of life in all its aspects: it is the norm of every norm, the premise of all other rules."

a way that is mostly individual, even though Teresa drew into her experience the whole of her spiritual family.

But the moment has come, at least this is our specific vocation, to discover, illuminate, build up, also an "exterior castle."

We see all of the Focolare Movement as an exterior castle, where Christ is present and gives light to all its parts, from its center to its periphery.

And if we consider that this new spirituality God has given to today's Church reaches both civil and ecclesiastical leaders, we realize immediately that this charism can transform not only the Work of Mary but also the entire body of society and of the Church into an exterior castle.

Key Points
of the Spirituality of Unity

We will begin by reviewing the various points of our collective spirituality in order to live them with deeper awareness and greater responsibility. Now that they have been written in our Statutes,[1] they are an expression, for us, of the will of God. We will look at them with a specific purpose in mind. As we praise God for having given them to us at a time when the world around us needed it, we will try to show how each point is truly a manifestation and a pillar of our collective spirituality. We will try to see how each one requires of those who live it that "something more" our collective spirituality calls for, that is, the giving and receiving involved in love and in unity.

We will examine these points on the basis of what we think the Holy Spirit suggested to us when we understood them for the first time.

Thus, we will use our writings, letters, etc., especially those from the early days of our Movement.

God-Love: Source of Unity

God-Love is the first point of our spirituality. Today, decades away from that first manifestation of God who

---

1. Statutes of the Work of Mary, article 8.

is Love, we realize more fully what a great gift it was, not only then for us first Focolarine, but also for the millions of people who later met the Movement, and how it is a gift for humanity in our time.

In re-reading material relevant to that event and seeing it in its historical context, we can also understand how necessary it was.

Not only had people been affected by the dramatic events of World War II, which sowed destruction and death, but in a more interior manner, they were affected by an atheistic and secularized vision of life and of the world. This had gradually evolved either into the absolute negation of God and consequently of the human being or in the painful quest for the meaning of one's existence, and in any case in the criticism of an image of God as static, uncaring, and far away.

Therefore, in the mind of Christians, in their way of thinking and acting, the reality of God-Love, announced by John the Apostle, was no longer so alive. And much less present — particularly in the West — was the rich doctrine developed from this central mystery of our faith by the Fathers of the Church like Augustine, Basil, Gregory of Nyssa, Maximus the Confessor, among others, and the great theologians of the Middle Ages, like Bernard of Clairvaux, Thomas Aquinas, Bonaventure, Duns Scotus, and others.

Certainly, there were stupendous writings through which countless saints and mystics of the Church, in both East and West, shared with us their union with God and their experience of his infinite love. They confirmed and illustrated the progressive in-depth exploration that the Church, guided by the Holy Spirit, was making into the reality of God-Love, and they remained precious spiritual nourishment for every age. Yet, they reflected — as we have noted in the preceding chapter — a spirituality that was mostly individual, and for this reason was not suited to the new spiritual needs of our time, which is characterized by more interpersonal relationships and by interdependence among peoples.

THE FIRST INSPIRING SPARK

It was precisely in this context that the Lord revealed to us anew, through the charism of unity, God as love, thus enkindling what John Paul II described as the "first inspiring spark."[2]

It should be said that, because of my previous Christian formation, I was prepared to accept the reality of God-Love as part of my faith. But, along with other circumstances that forcefully highlighted this reality during those days, the words, "God loves you immensely," addressed to me as we know,[3] brought this reality to the forefront within me. And it is important to point out that it did not impact only me. On the contrary! It immediately became the common heritage of many.

---

2. *Insegnamenti di Giovanni Paolo II* VII/2 (Rome: Libreria Editrice Vaticana, 1984), pp. 223–225.

3. The author is referring to an episode that is well known within the Focolare, and one that she has related many times: "During those days a priest asked me to offer a part of my day to God. Moved by youthful generosity, I responded: 'Even the whole day!' The priest was impressed, had me kneel down, gave me his blessing, and said to me: 'God loves you immensely.' These words, spoken by a man to whom God had given spiritual authority over others, had a great effect on me. What I had learned as a Christian already as a little girl, namely, that God is love, that he knows me, that — as Jesus says — he even counts the hairs of my head, entered into my mind and heart in a manner that was completely new, as if it were a lightning bolt: 'God loves me! God is Love!'" (Chiara Lubich, *Incontri con l'Oriente* [Rome: Città Nuova, 1987], pp. 20–21).

I wrote later on: "I am saying this, I am repeating it to my friends: 'God loves us immensely.' 'God loves you immensely.' " Since that moment we first Focolarine perceived God present everywhere with his love: throughout the day, in our enthusiasm, in our resolutions, in joyful and comforting events, in situations that were sad, awkward, or difficult.

He was always there, he was present everywhere. And he explained to us that everything is love: all that we were and all that concerned us; that we were his children and he was our Father; that nothing escaped his love, not even our mistakes, because he permitted them; that his love enveloped Christians such as us, the Church, the world, and the entire universe.

Thus, something new flashed through our mind: God is love. And this absolute novelty made us realize that God was no longer distant, inaccessible, foreign to our life; on the contrary, he was reaching out to me, to us, with the immensity of his love. God-Love emerged in our hearts as the most real and true of all realities. And, while the war showed all things to be precarious and transitory, we chose him as the ideal of our lives.

The response that God elicited from that first group of Focolarine was equally immediate and meaningful.

A letter written in 1944 communicates the atmosphere of those early days and describes the infusion of light and fire through which God-Love became present in our lives, and — this is interesting — it already shows the intuition we had of the very profound bond it would bring about among us:

"You have been blinded with me by the fiery brilliance of an ideal that exceeds all things and contains all things: by the infinite love of God!

"It is he, my God and your God, who has established a bond between us that is stronger than death."

God-Love was therefore the living source of the unity that the Work of Mary is called upon to live and to show to others, so as to contribute to the fulfillment of Jesus' last prayer. Believing in God's love — which he himself "revealed" to us ("We have known and believe the love God has for us," 1 Jn 4:16) — was the starting point of our spirituality, which was already characterized by unity. Thus, it appeared as a collective spirituality.

The Closer We Come to God, the Closer We Come to One Another

God's will is the second point. To God, who loves each one of us immensely, we respond by seeking to love him immensely. We felt that we would have no meaning in the world if we were not a little flame of this infinite fire: love that responds to Love.

But how could we do this?

We read in a letter from 1943: "Love him! Listen to what he wants from you in every moment of your life. Do this with all your heart."

Therefore, to love God means to do his will.

From the beginning of our new way of life we used the image of the sun with its rays to illustrate how we wanted to live God's will. We find this described in another letter from those days:

"Look at the sun and its rays.

"The sun is a symbol of the will of God, which is God himself.

"The rays are the will of God for each individual.

"Walk towards the sun in the light of your ray, different and distinct from every other ray, and fulfill the particular, wonderful plan God wants from you.

"There is an infinite number of rays, all coming from the same sun: a single will, particular for each person. The closer the rays come to the sun, the closer they come to one another.

"We too . . . the closer we come to God, by doing the will of God more and more perfectly, the closer we come to one another.

"Until we are all one!"[4]

All one. Each one of us doing God's will makes us all one.

To reach this goal, of being one, we exhorted everyone to say his or her own vigorous, total, determined yes to God's will.

"With all the ardor of our hearts let us say yes to God's will always. . . .

"If we all do God's will, we will very soon be *that perfect unity* that Jesus wants on earth as in heaven! . . .

"I invite you all to do this because God has placed a magnificent star upon each one of us — his particular will for each of us — and by following it, we will all reach heaven *united,* and we will see many other stars following in the wake of our own light!"[5]

"When God's will is done on earth as in heaven, the testament of Jesus will be fulfilled."[6]

---

4. Chiara Lubich, 27 October 1947, in *Meditations* (London: New City, 2005), p. 26; cf. also *Christian Living Today* (Hyde Park, NY: New City Press, 1997), pp. 51–52.
5. Chiara Lubich, Letter, Christmas 1946, in *Our Yes to God* (Brooklyn, NY: New City Press, 1981), pp. 95–96.
6. Chiara Lubich, 27 October 1947, from the letter quoted above.

Also this second cornerstone of our spirituality — doing God's will — which at first glance may seem to be the expression of an individual spirituality — is revealed to us by our charism with a marked collective dimension, with that "something more" as compared to other spiritualities in which the individual aspect seems to prevail over the communitarian one.

In the more individual spiritualities, in fact, it is usually each Christian personally who, by fulfilling the divine will evermore perfectly, reaches union with God, even to the point of transformation in Christ.[7]

By living God's will according to our spirituality, which springs from the charism of unity, we see that we become more united not only with God but also with one another. Thus we are transformed personally and collectively into Christ.

This link between God's will and unity is beautifully illustrated by Peter Chrysologus:

> "Your will be done, on earth as it is in heaven" (Mt 6:10). On earth as it is in heaven. Everything will be heaven, then; the one mind of God will guide everyone; all will be in Christ and Christ will be in all, when everyone will savor and carry out only God's will. Then *all will be one, indeed, one single [Christ], in all.*[8]

---

7. Cf. Teresa of Avila, *The Way of Perfection*, chap. 32; and John of the Cross, *The Ascent of Mount Carmel* II, 5, 3–4; *The Living Flame of Love* 3, 68.
8. Peter Chrysologus, *Sermons*, 72: *PL* 52, 406.

To Love and To Be Loved

The third point is *love of neighbor*. The will of God is God, and God is love. His will, therefore, is love, and he wants us to love too. He wants us to love him with all our heart, all our soul, and all our mind, and to love every neighbor as ourselves (cf. Mt 22:37–39).

We, too, had to be love in life: little suns beside the Sun.

At that time, the word "love" usually indicated either the natural sentiment that links a man and a woman or eroticism. It was not normally used in religious terminology, where the preferred term was "charity," but often with the limited meaning of almsgiving. The singular manifestation of God-Love that we had received, and our direct contact with the Word of God, re-focused our attention on the Christian meaning of love.

Indeed, we immediately sensed that love was the very core of the Christian message and, as such, it was our absolute duty to put it into practice.

We began by loving the poor. But quite soon, because of this practice (since love brings light) we understood that we had to love everyone.

But how could we do this? By serving, which the Spirit soon explained to us with the words "making ourselves one."

I wrote: "Making ourselves one with every person we meet. This means sharing their feelings, carrying their burdens, making their problems our own and solving them as if they were ours, because love has *made* them ours.

"We must make ourselves one in everything except sin.

"This is what Paul meant when he said: 'I made myself all things to all people' (1 Cor 9:22).

"Making ourselves one requires constantly dying to ourselves. Yet, it is for this very reason that when others are loved in this way, sooner or later they are won over by Christ who lives in us through the death of our ego."[9]

When this happens, the other person responds to our love with his or her own love, and love of neighbor grows to the point of becoming mutual.

In another writing, we find: "See Jesus in every person you meet in each moment of the day, from morning till night.

"If your eye is clear, it is God seeing through you. And God is love, and love wants to unite, by winning over the other. . . .

"Look outside yourself, not at yourself, not at things, not at people; look at God outside yourself in order to unite yourself to him.

"He is in the depths of every soul that has life; if a soul has no life, it is like a tabernacle of God waiting to achieve the meaning and joy of its existence.

"Look at every neighbor with love, and loving is giving. But one gift calls for another, and you will be loved.

"Thus, love is loving and being loved, as in the Trinity.

"And God in you will capture hearts, lighting up in them the Trinity, already present perhaps through grace, but inactive. . . .

---

9. Cf. Chiara Lubich, "Unity, The Longing of Our Times" in *Living City* 6:1983, p. 7.

"Look then at your neighbor and give yourself to your neighbor in order to give yourself to Jesus, and Jesus will give himself to you. It is the law of love: 'Give and gifts will be given to you.'

"Let yourself be consumed by the other person — out of love for Jesus. Let yourself be 'eaten' — as another eucharist. Put yourself completely at the other's service, which means at the service of God, and your neighbor will come to you and will love you. . . .

"Love is a fire that penetrates hearts and makes them perfectly one.

"Then within yourself, you will no longer find yourself, or your brother or sister; you will find Love, which is God living within you.

"And Love will go out to love other brothers and sisters because, now that your eye is clear, it will find Him in them, and *all will be one*. . . ."[10]

And "all will be one." Not just any kind of love, then. No, the kind of love that brings about unity.

Reciprocity, therefore, and unity: the "something more" of our collective spirituality in another of its points.

Being "Living Words" So As to Be One

The Word of Life is the fourth point. Having discovered the uniqueness and universality of the Words of God, while we were still in the air-raid shelters, we felt the desire to translate them into life, one by one. This was the beginning of a practice that continues today, more than fifty years later, and that will never end.

---

10. Chiara Lubich, Unpublished Writing, November 1949.

I wrote in 1948:

"We have understood that the world needs to be cured by the gospel, because only the Good News can give back to the world the life it lacks.

"This is why we live the *Word of Life*. . . .

"We *make it flesh* in ourselves to the point of being that living Word. All the words of the gospel are equal to each other since they all contain the truth, just as a tiny piece of the sacred host contains Jesus.

"One word would be enough to make one a saint, another Jesus.

"And all of us can live the word, whatever our vocation, age, gender, or background, because Jesus is light for every person who comes into this world. . . .

"Only in this way: only in doing the truth do we love! Otherwise, love is empty sentimentalism.

"Let us be living gospels, living words of life, another Jesus! . . . and we will imitate Mary, Mother of the Light, of the Word: the living Word.

"We have no other book except the gospel; no other science, no other art.

"That is where life is! 'Whoever finds it never dies.' "[11]

And quite soon we understood that living the Word makes us one with each other.

"Although we are far from one another, some in the mountains and others by the sea, a light will join us together. It is a light that the senses cannot grasp and is unknown to the world, but it is more precious to God . . . than anything else: the Word of Life.

_____

11. Chiara Lubich, Unpublished Letter, 17 August 1948.

"We can be *one* only on condition that each of us is another Jesus: a living Word of God."[12]

Using the example of the grafting of plants, where two branches stripped of their bark are united since they are "alive," we said:

"When can two souls be truly living in unity? When they are 'alive,' that is, when they are stripped of all that is merely human . . . when they have lived and incarnated the Word of Life so that they become living words. Two living words can be consumed into one. If one of them is not alive, the other one cannot be united with it."[13]

But the "something more" in this point of our collective spirituality — that is, reciprocity and unity — comes into full relief if we consider a practice we had and still have today in living the gospel Words.

It is not enough to live them on our own.

No, we need to share our experiences of the Word of Life with one another. In this way, we are evangelized, that is, transformed into another Christ because of the effort we make to live in this way, and because of all we do to receive within ourselves the light and experience of others. Thus we evangelize ourselves as individuals and as a community. We become more and more Jesus, individually and collectively.

The Law of Heaven

Mutual love is the fifth point. As we have already seen, love of neighbor, making ourselves one with the others,

---

12. Chiara Lubich, Unpublished Letter, June 1949.
13. Chiara Lubich, Unpublished Letter, 23 October 1948.

led the initial group of Focolarine to mutual love, the heart of the gospel: "Just as I have loved you, you also should love one another" (Jn 13:34).

Taking the words "as I have loved you" literally, declaring that we are ready to give our lives for one another, and ready to give up anything for our brothers and sisters as Jesus did in his abandonment out of love for us, even to the point of feeling that he had lost his union with God, made of these words the typical commandment of our collective spirituality. It contained the required "something more": mutual giving and receiving and, as we shall see, unity.

At various times in the history of the Church, the holy founders and their disciples referred to this commandment in their Rules.

The Rule of Augustine, for example, says: "The main reason you are gathered in the same house is to live in harmony and to be united in mind and heart as you strive toward God."[14]

Saint Benedict's Rule: "Seek to be first in honoring each other . . . competing in mutual obedience; let no one seek his own interests, but rather that of the others; offer fraternal charity with pure love."[15]

And the Rule of Francis: "Let them love one another, as the Lord says: *This is my commandment: that you love one another as I have loved you.* Let them express the love they have for one another by their deeds, as the Apostle says: *Let us love not in word or speech but in deed and truth.* . . . Let them not consider the least sins of others. Instead, let

---

14. Saint Augustine, *Rule* I, 3.
15. Saint Benedict, *Rule for Monasteries* LXXII.

them reflect more upon their own sins *in the bitterness of their soul.*"[16]

However, what we notice in these splendid Rules is that — it would seem — the word "as" in "*as* I have loved you" has not always been given much explicit consideration.

From the earliest days of the Focolare, looking to our model Jesus crucified and forsaken (this is our measure, the "as"), we understood that faithfulness to mutual love would bring about unity according to the life of the Trinity.

"Do you know to what point we must love one another?" we said one day, still unaware of Jesus' last prayer. "To the point of being consumed in one."[17] Like God who, being love, is Three and One.

At that time I wrote: "Jesus really brought the 'law of heaven' to earth. . . .

"It is the life of the Most Holy Trinity that we must try to imitate by loving one another, with the grace of God, as the Persons of the Most Holy Trinity love one another."[18]

And the dynamism of the intra-trinitarian life is the unconditional mutual gift of self; it is total and eternal communion ("All that is mine is yours and all that is yours is mine," Jn 17:10) between the Father and the Son in the Spirit.

---

16. "The Earlier Rule" (The Rule without a Papal Seal) XI, in Francis of Assisi: Early Documents, vol. 1: *The Saint* (Hyde Park, NY: New City Press, 1999), p. 72.

17. Chiara Lubich, "Unità e comunità" I. "La comunità cristiana," in *Fides,* October 1948, p. 4.

18. Chiara Lubich, "Sintesi della spiritualità," in *Mariapoli* '68, Rome, 1968, p. 76.

A similar reality, we felt, is imprinted by God in the relationships among people. We wrote then: "I felt that I have been created as a gift for the person next to me, and the person next to me has been created by God as a gift for me. Just as the Father in the Trinity is everything for the Son, and the Son is everything for the Father."[19] And "The relationship among us is the Holy Spirit, the same relationship that exists among the Persons of the Trinity."[20]

The Key to Unity: Jesus Forsaken

Jesus Forsaken is the sixth point. Jesus Forsaken, as we have said many times, is the "something more" *of* the Passion and *in* the Passion. Jesus had lost his disciples and his mother; his life was being brutally drained from him through the scourging, the crown of thorns, the nails, the blood he shed, through being hung on the cross.

All he had left was his union with God, his Father. He consented to losing, to renouncing that too: "My God, my God, why have you forsaken me?" (Mt 27:46). And he sacrificed himself in this way out of love for us.

His abandonment is a "something more," and through our spirituality we know that it leads — as is stated in our Statutes (art. 8) — to that "outer and inner renunciation" necessary for every form of unity.

We understood all this as early as 24 January 1944 when, not even two months after the date we consider

19. Marisa Cerini, *God Who is Love* (New York: New City Press, 1991), p. 52.
20. Ibid.

to be the beginning of the Focolare, 7 December 1943, through a well-known incident[21] we discovered this suffering of Jesus. On that day, 24 January, we decided to give ourselves to him, as to the greatest love.

In Jesus Forsaken — we would soon understand — we contemplated the "key to unity."

Several letters bear witness to this. Here are three excerpts:

"Is it not understood yet . . . that the greatest ideal a human heart can yearn for — unity — is a distant dream and a mirage if those who want it do not set their hearts exclusively upon Jesus, who was forsaken by all, even by his Father?"

Another:

---

21. " . . . the encounter with Jesus forsaken at Dori [Zamboni]'s house, an encounter which this time we will let her describe herself.

"She tells: 'We went in search of the poor and it was probably from them that I caught an infection on my face. I was covered with sores. The medicines I took did not halt the disease. But, with my face appropriately protected, I kept on going to Mass and to our Saturday meetings.

" 'It was cold, and to go outside under such conditions could have been bad for me. Since my family would not let me go out, Chiara asked a Capuchin priest to bring me Communion. While I was making my thanksgiving after receiving the eucharist, the priest asked Chiara what in her opinion was the moment of Jesus' greatest suffering during his passion. She replied she had always heard that it was the pain he felt in the Garden of Gethsemane. Then the priest remarked: "But I believe, rather, that it was what he felt on the cross, when he cried out: 'My God, my God, why have you forsaken me?' (Mt 47:26)."

" 'As soon as the priest left, I turned to Chiara. Having overheard their conversation, I felt sure she would give me an explanation. Instead, she said: "If Jesus' greatest pain was his abandonment by his Father, we will choose him as our Ideal and that is the way we will follow him" ' " (Chiara Lubich, *Jesus: The Heart of His Message, Unity and Jesus Forsaken* [Hyde Park: New City Press, 1985], pp. 45–46).

"It is only by loving Jesus Forsaken with all your heart, him whose body is all wound and whose soul is all darkness, that you will be formed in unity."[22]

And finally:

"He is everything! If the world only knew him! If souls who pursue unity would only welcome him as their only goal, as their everything, then unity would suffer no fluctuations; it would never break."[23]

Still other letters give further witness:

"I am convinced that in its most spiritual aspect, at its deepest and most intimate level, unity can be understood only by a person who has chosen as their portion of life . . . Jesus forsaken, crying out 'My God, my God, why have you forsaken me?'

"All light on unity flows from that cry.

"To choose him as our only goal, our only objective, the point of arrival for our own life is . . . to generate an infinite number of souls into unity."[24]

"What is he missing in his anguished state?

"What is the medicine that can heal his pain?

"*God*!

"It is God that is missing.

"How can we give him God?

"If we are united we will have him in our midst, and the Jesus who will be born of our unity will console our crucified Love!"[25]

---

22. Chiara Lubich, Letter, 2 February 1949, in *Jesus: The Heart of His Message*, p. 60.
23. Chiara Lubich, Unpublished Letter, 23 April 1948.
24. Chiara Lubich, Letter, 30 March 1948, in *Jesus: The Heart of His Message*, pp. 58–59.
25. Chiara Lubich, Letter, 1 April 1948, in *Jesus: The Heart of His Message*, p. 65.

Unity

Unity is the seventh point. It is a cornerstone of our spirituality because it expresses, even by itself, what the Spirit wants from us.

Indeed, in it the "something more" of our spiritual way of living, when compared to others, is more than evident. This is true simply because those who live other, more individually accented, spiritualities do not always consciously strive, as something essential, toward unity with their brothers and sisters, as they do toward unity with God.

Unity instead requires this "something more," because it presumes a communion of at least two persons.

Unity is a grace that Jesus asked of the Father: "May all be one. As you, Father, are in me and I am in you, may they also be in us" (Jn 17:21). And since it is a grace, we cannot attain it through our own efforts. We need, however, to prepare ourselves so that we can receive it: by loving one another as Jesus loved us. And what must be emphasized here is what "as" means: with the measure of the forsakenness of Jesus. Jesus, in fact, loved in this way and to this point. Thus, it is not enough to love one another in just any way — for example as friends, who immediately understand one another or who exchange gestures of kindness. Material and spiritual detachment is needed on both sides in order to "make ourselves one" with one another. This is the best preparation for obtaining the grace of unity.

For this point too, after investigating writings and documents from the early days to see what our charism taught us about unity, and how we considered it, we came up with a few passages.

I wrote in 1947:

"Fix in your mind one single idea.

"It was always one single idea that produced the great saints.

"And our idea is this: Unity."[26]

And this — I add now — holds true also for the present.

In another letter, from 1948, I wrote:

"Let everything else go, but Unity never! . . .

"Always bring among you . . . this blazing Fire.

"Don't be afraid to die. You've learned already by experience that Unity requires all to die, to give life to the One. . . .

"Do this as a sacrosanct *duty*, even if it will also bring you immense joy!

"Jesus promised the fullness of joy to those who live in unity! . . ."[27]

Unity, unity, I add now, and certainly not to close ourselves in but to open ourselves up as the gospel asks.

The letter continues by saying:

"Let's make Unity among us, which gives us the fullness of joy, peace, and strength, the springboard for rushing to . . . wherever there is no unity and to bring it there."[28]

And another:

". . . as long as all are not one, are not Jesus, we cannot sit back and rest. We must always be on the front line in the struggle against ourselves and evil, hating Satan and the world. We must feel that every lack of unity around

26. Chiara Lubich, Letter, New Year's Day 1947; in *Jesus: The Heart of His Message*, p. 36 (translation revised).
27. Letter, 1 April in *Jesus: The Heart of His Message*, p. 32.
28. *Jesus: The Heart of His Message*, p. 35.

us is a grave responsibility that weighs on our soul. Jesus, often, is present in people's hearts, but buried. Living the fullest unity among us, we must bring such a Light that it will enchant everyone. Then they will search for it within themselves and allow it to shine forth."[29]

Jesus Among Us

Then we immediately discover what unity offers. And here we pass on to the eighth point: unity offers Jesus in our midst. Here again, the "something more" is evident. There must be at least two of us in order to have him among us, and two of us united in his name, that is, in his love.

Jesus among us. He is the grace that we obtain in unity. It is a super-grace because it is Jesus himself.

The presence of Jesus among us is a directive of his to be lived ("Where two or more . . ."), and it is Jesus himself who gives it.

This presence of Jesus is surprisingly up-to-date. We know that often it is difficult in our day to speak of Jesus because he is seen as someone far away, someone who lived two thousand years ago, who is superseded, perhaps of a former world. That Jesus is still alive today, that he journeys with us through history, as he promised when he said "I am with you always, to the end of the age" (Mt 28:20), is no longer understood today. And this is due to the secularized, materialistic, and indifferent environment that has had an influence even on the Church itself.

---

29. Chiara Lubich, Letter, 4 January 1949.

Instead, if we bring him into our midst, many will be able to meet him now, two thousand years later.

Jesus in our midst is really the effect of unity. This is what I wrote in a page that expresses our surprise at these first discoveries, as well as our excitement and joy.

"Unity!

"Who would dare speak of it?

"It is ineffable like God!

"You feel it, see it, enjoy it but . . . it is ineffable!

"Everyone rejoices in its presence, everyone suffers from its absence.

"It is peace, joy, love, ardor, the atmosphere of heroism, of the highest generosity.

"It is Jesus among us!"[30]

And the letter continues:

"Jesus among us! To live so as to have him always with us, so as to bring him to a world so unaware of his peace, so as to carry within ourselves his light! His light!

"I would like to speak to you, but I don't know how. . . .

"The mind contemplates, satiated by beauty!

"I would prefer to let the whole world go to pieces, so long as he is always with us, among us who are united in his name because dead to ourselves!

"Brothers, our Lord has given us a magnificent ideal . . . let us stick to it faithfully, at whatever cost, even if some day our souls might have to cry out in the torment of infinite pain: 'My God, my God, why have you too forsaken me?'

---

30. Letter, 29 April 1948 in *The Secret of Unity* (London: New City, 1985), p. 27; cf. *Jesus: The Heart of His Message*, p. 28.

"Let's go ahead, not counting on our own petty and limited strength, but on the omnipotence of Unity.

"I have had firsthand experiences of how God among us works the impossible. . . .

"If we stick faithfully to our commitment ('that all may be one') the world will see Unity. . . .

"And don't be afraid to give up everything for Unity; unless we love . . . beyond all measure, unless we lose our own judgment and our own desires, we shall never be one! . . .

"Unity above all, in all, after all! Arguments don't count for much, nor do the holiest of discussions, unless we give life to Jesus among us. . . ."[31]

The following passage, too, is from 1948:

"These past few days . . . it occurred to me, I felt in my soul, that Unity is not made up of focolare houses, of being near to one another or far. . . . It is Something above all these things. It is the Peace of Heaven, it is full-ness of Joy, perfect Light that illumines the darkest night, it is the most ardent and pure love. . . it is *Jesus*. . . .

"And unity, this Something intangible, untouchable, invisible, rises up and asserts itself! It is all spiritual, all Spirit. But it is *real, concrete; it satisfies the soul and makes it sing.*

"What a Way the Lord has given to us! What a wonder! What a gift!"[32]

Jesus in the midst of the world, among the Christian people . . . among nations. This promise of his, which down the centuries was realized perhaps in convents and monasteries, and highlighted for our times by

---

31. Chiara Lubich, Letter, 29 April 1948 in Judith Povilus, *United in His Name* (Hyde Park, NY: New City Press, 1992), p. 18.
32. Unpublished Letter, 15 June 1948.

Vatican II, has now become, through our Movement, something accessible for all people.

Let's listen again to what we said about him when he manifested himself and how, even then, we felt the need to make him known.

"The happiness that we feel in unity, which you have given us through your death, is something we want to give all the souls that touch ours. We cannot reserve it to ourselves, seeing that there are so many . . . who feel hunger and thirst for this complete peace, this boundless joy. . . ."[33]

We had such great esteem for him in our midst that in another well-known passage we wrote:

"If we are united, Jesus is among us. And this has value. It is worth more than any other treasure that our heart may possess; more than mother, father, brothers, sisters, children. It is worth more than our house, our work, or our property; more than the works of art in a great city like Rome; more than our business deals; more than nature which surrounds us with flowers and fields, the sea and the stars; more than our own soul.

"It is he who, inspiring his saints with his eternal truths, leaves his mark upon every age.

"This too is his hour. Not so much the hour of a saint but of him, of him among us . . .

But we must enlarge Christ. . . . Make one of all and in all the One."

In later years, when we had already begun to look more closely, even though in a different way, at these cornerstones of our spirituality, we said:

_____

33. Letter, 27 December 1948, in _Jesus: The Heart of His Message_, p. 34.

"We all know that the great choice of the Focolare and of each one of us was the choice of God. . . . We adored him present in the tabernacles, we loved him in our neighbors, we contemplated him beyond the stars in the immensity of the universe.

"But one day we were surprised by the thought that such a God who was so close to us with his love, but so far away from us with his majesty, had come down to be near us when we were united, setting his dwelling place among us. . . .

"Jesus in our midst: brother among his brothers and sisters, teacher, guide, comfort, light; we have no cause to envy those who lived with him in Palestine. We can hope for everything from this tremendous presence. He is the source of a divine blaze of fire wherever he is in the world, for he said, 'I came to bring fire to the earth' (Lk 12:49).

"We have a huge treasure, we have *the* treasure."[34]

Another passage:

"When we were united . . . we felt all the power of Jesus among us. It was as if we were all clothed in the power and blessing of heaven. We felt capable of the noblest actions for God, the most ardent and difficult resolutions, which we were then able to carry out; whereas before, when alone, for all our good will, it was difficult to fully live up to the promises we had made to the Lord. We felt a power that wasn't merely human."[35]

Jesus in our midst — he cannot help but do great things because he is Jesus.

---

34. Chiara Lubich, *When Our Love is Charity*. Spiritual Writings, vol. 2 (Hyde Park, NY: New City Press, 1991), pp. 46, 53 (translation revised).

35. *When Our Love is Charity*, pp. 54–55.

Jesus in our midst — he enables us to obtain everything through praying the *"consenserint."*[36]

Jesus in our midst is an everlasting Christmas in the world, an everlasting Easter, because the risen Lord is constantly alive among us.

Jesus in our midst is the treasure we must leave to those who follow us, with the exhortation to keep him present through the new commandment and unity.

The Eucharist

And now the *eucharist.*

Where is the "something more" in the eucharist?

It is quickly said. The eucharist can be seen (and many Christians do see it only in this way) simply as food that nourishes our soul spiritually, to be received at least once a year or on feast days or on Sundays, or even daily. Since, however, the eucharist is our Lord in person, whom we adore and to whom we pray, in the Focolare Movement we have always seen the eucharist also for what it produces: unity. And this is the "something more."

It is the eucharist that gives us that grace that we should expect when we live the new commandment, where we experience unity, Jesus in our midst.

But even before we became acquainted with this quality of the eucharist (that is, the bond of unity), the Holy Spirit was aware of it, and because he had called us to the ideal of unity, he urged us to be nourished by the body and blood of Christ.

---

36. The Latin term means "agree" and is from Matthew 18:19: ". . . if two of you agree on earth about anything you ask, it will be done for you by my Father in heaven."

Just as newborn babes instinctively feed at their mothers' breasts without knowing what they are doing, we noted something that happened from the very beginning of the Focolare: those who got to know us began to receive Holy Communion every day.

How can we explain this?

What instinct is for the newborn baby, the Holy Spirit is for adults who have been born anew into the life that the gospel of unity brings. They are carried into the "heart" of the Church their mother, where they feed on the most precious nectar she has.

Moreover, we became aware of one thing quite soon. It seemed indicative to us that Jesus, speaking to the Father in his famous prayer, asked for unity among his followers and among those who would come later, *after* having instituted the eucharist.

Unity, therefore, reaches its fullness through the eucharist.

Unity can be lived fully only through the eucharist, which makes us not only one through love, but one body and one blood with Christ and with each other.

The Church

If it is the *Church* that makes the eucharist, then it is the eucharist that makes the *Church* and makes it communion.

In this affirmation lies the reason for the "something more" in our consideration of the Church.

At the time when the Focolare began, the Church was often seen only as a stone structure, with Jesus in the tabernacle, and with Mary, Saint Anthony or another saint above the altar . . . the Church was, in a certain sense, for many people taken as being the same things as the catechism, First Communion. . . . It also meant the other sacraments, as well as patronal festivals; perhaps it meant belonging to Catholic Action groups, and so on. It meant the parish and the parish priest and, if people were aware of their existence, the bishop and the pope.

Through the charism of unity and all that goes with it, we understood that while the Church may be all of this, more than anything else, in the depths of its being, it is the people of God. It is communion: the Church-communion.

Then, Vatican II defined it this way, and this brought about a revolution.

What does it mean to live the Church as communion?

It means creating bonds of love among all those who are part of it: among its members, its various subdivisions (parishes, dioceses, movements, structures, councils, commissions, and so on); with other things that are in some way linked to the Church (other Churches, other religions which are connected with the Church through the presence of the "seeds of the Word," and other cultures with the values they bring).

Our spirituality teaches and helps us to practice all of this.

It also means that persons in positions of responsibility create bonds of love with the faithful, so that each command may be prepared by love (making those in charge into people who "preside in love").

Moreover, the faithful should build bonds of love with those in positions of responsibility. This is documented by the following letters, which show that the Focolare's relationship with the Church was also marked by communion.

I wrote in 1969:

"This was not only out of a principle of obedience to the Church or simply from fear of heresy! It was actually the Church which was drawing us to itself. Or better still, it was the Holy Spirit in us who urged us to be united with the Holy Spirit who is in the Church, because it is one and the same Holy Spirit."[37]

The following sentence is from our early years:

"The Focolarini see the Church as a family in which each member has to retain his or her own position and vocation, but all should feel they are brothers and sisters, through love in Christ Jesus."[38]

And everything is done in obedience to whoever has the charism of authority. In fact, we owe the Church an obedient love, a love that is then reciprocated, as we have always experienced.

We have consistently had this attitude toward bishops.

We wrote back in 1947:

" 'Who hears you hears me' (Lk 10:16).

"Our souls, caught up by the voices of this world, need so much to hear the voice of Christ!

"But you must not expect Christ to descend on earth to speak to you. When he was here on earth, he appointed his ministers: those who were to carry on in his place.

"Go to them with faith!

"You are fighting a battle for the triumph of the spirit over matter, the triumph of the supernatural. . . . Look

---

37. Chiara Lubich, *Servants of All* (Brooklyn, NY: New City Press, 1978), p. 85; cf. also *Servants of All* (London: New City, 1979), 54.

38. Chiara Lubich, Unpublished Writing, *How the Work of Mary relates to people who do not belong to it.*

at the minister — whoever he is — as someone who speaks on behalf of Jesus, without regard to his possible imperfections. His word is the word of God.

" 'Who hears you hears me'!

"Jesus wants to be listened to through his ministers. This is the way he established it; this is the way it is."[39]

And in 1952:

"We must neither argue nor hesitate. We are one only in the divine will, and that is expressed by the bishop."[40]

". . . only in this way, in unity among us and with the Church, will our ideal invade the earth and be an invasion of love."[41]

In 1956:

"From experience we can say that bishops are different from other people. One senses it when one tells them about our spirituality, or when they speak. Their words have a weight and fervor that immediately distinguishes them from even the holiest priest or theologian.

"Moreover, they have the grace to get to the point of the matter, and to explain it amply. It is their charism."[42]

In 1960 I said:

"I wish that all would feel that they have a mother, and that this mother is always there to nourish them. And I wish that everyone would seek this genuine milk that is given by the Holy Father and the bishops, and that they would drink it and make it their own."[43]

---

39. Chiara Lubich, *Servants of All*, pp. 79–80.
40. *Servants of All*, p. 80.
41. Chiara Lubich, Letter, 14 February 1952.
42. *Servants of All*, p. 81.
43. *Servants of All*, p. 82.

Thus one day a sort of hymn sprang from our hearts:

"The Church, our most pure mother, has received us into her family, opening for us, through her priests and sacraments, the gates of the true paradise.

"She has forged us as soldiers of Christ.

"She has forgiven us and canceled our sins seventy times seven.

"She has nourished us with the Body of Jesus and has given a divine seal to the love of our fathers and mothers.

"She has raised a number of poor created beings like us to the exalted dignity of the priesthood.

"Finally, she will give us the last farewell; she will put us on our way to God. She will give us God.

"Unless our hearts sing her praises, they are withered organs.

"Unless our minds see and admire her, they are blind and dark.

"Unless we speak of her, our words might as well dry up on our lips."[44]

Mary

And now we come to Mary.

Let us see, first of all, how Mary, who is considered to be one of the main points of our spirituality, contains that "something more."

Reflecting on the way we thought of Mary before the experience in our Movement, and attributing this, in some measure, to the more individualistic spiritualities,

---

44. Chiara Lubich, *Stirrings of Unity* (Queens, NY: New City Press, 1964), p. 12.

we could say that there was a great love, an enormous devotion for the Virgin Mary, Mother of God, for whom shrines, at times elaborate, have been erected all over the world. The rosary was the preferred prayer, which she herself often recommended; people willingly participated in the popular celebrations of her various feast days; the month of May was especially honored; at times, people "consecrated themselves" to her, as they used to say; and the elderly, in particular, wished to die with her name on their lips. These are many different aspects of a deeply-felt devotion, but — I repeat — a predominately individual one.

In the Focolare experience, there is "something more."

In fact, while she is loved for all her splendid attributes, such as the Immaculate One, the *Theotokos*, the One Assumed into heaven, and is admired as the "Word fully lived," the "Woman of Love," the "Daughter of the Father," she is not only venerated and invoked but imitated and, in a certain way, re-lived as the Mother of Unity, which means the mother not only of individual Christians, but of the Church as a whole.

She is the mother of unity, mother of the Church, in the moment of her desolation, similar and next to Jesus Forsaken, as she gives her second yes. In her own way, she too is forsaken.

For us, Mary Desolate does not only stand for a masterpiece of virtue, which she is. Mary Desolate is the one who, with Jesus crucified and forsaken, gave her own contribution toward the redemption of the human race and became our mother in John.

In that moment, she co-generated another Christ, the Christ who formed his mystical body, and as mother she appears as the bond of unity among all. She unites her children, making them brothers and sisters, as the mothers around the world do.

And just as these children, whom she too has generated, have the features of Jesus, they have hers as well.

As we briefly look over the history of the Focolare Movement with regard to Mary, we can see more clearly who Mary is for us, and how she can be considered as a cornerstone of our spirituality.

From the earliest days of the Focolare, although during that period of time it seemed that she was letting the Spirit highlight almost exclusively Jesus and his gospel, Mary appeared, although discreetly, in order to reveal to us at once her relationship with unity.

Some examples.

I wrote in 1947:

"I am convinced that it is she [Mary] who wants unity. She [Mary]: *Mater unitatis!* . . .

"She knows Satan, his promises, deceptions, and traps; and she calls her children to be united, to help one another as they journey along the way of love!"[45]

Another letter from 1947:

"Our Lady wants us to be united in our journey! She knows that 'where two or more' are united in the holy name of her Son, he is in their midst! And where there is Jesus, dangers flee and obstacles disappear. . . . He overcomes everything because he is love!"[46]

Later on she manifested herself to our soul in all her splendor. We saw that her greatness was in proportion to how much she had lowered herself, to how much she had annulled herself.

---

45. Chiara Lubich, Unpublished Letter, 6 September 1947.
46. Chiara Lubich, Another Unpublished Letter, 6 September 1947.

In 1949, while we were together in the mountains, it seemed that the Lord showed us the main lines of the Work of Mary that would come to life.

We understood that, through it, Mary wanted in some way to return on earth.

This perception was so strong that in admiring her unique beauty and thinking of her and seeing her almost alone — because we couldn't find any children beside her worthy of such a mother, except for Jesus — we felt urged to ask her to bring about on earth a family of sons and daughters all like her.

Before that, we had asked Jesus in the eucharist to entrust us, to "consecrate" us to Mary, as he knows how.

We had understood that this act had not been merely an expression of devotion empty of true content, but that this "consecration" had brought about something new.

It seemed to us that Mary had clothed us with her immaculateness.

It seemed as if we were experiencing in our small group what Montfort spoke about with regard to the interior wonders that Mary secretly works in souls: "The principal effect is that Mary comes to live in the soul so that it is no longer the soul that lives, but Mary who lives in the soul."[47]

Essentially, it seemed that what Paul VI had asked one day had become a reality. He prayed: "Teach us what we already know . . . to be immaculate as you are."[48]

We felt ourselves to be children of Mary and — in a way that we will never be able to forget — for the first time, we felt that Mary was our mother.

---

47. L. G. Montfort, *Il Segreto di Maria*, n. 55.
48. *Insegnamenti di Paulo VI*, VII (Rome: Libreria Editrice Vaticana, 1969), pp. 685–688.

A few years later, the following well-known episode confirmed all this for us:

"I went into church one day, and with my heart full of trust, I asked: 'Why did you wish to remain on earth, on every point of the earth, in the most sweet Eucharist, and you have not found — you who are God — also a way to bring and to leave Mary here, the mother of all of us who journey?'

"In the silence he seemed to reply: 'I have not left her because I want to see her again in you.' "[49]

To be another Mary, a little Mary; to find in our mother what we are called to be and in ourselves the possibility to be another her.

But to be mother as she is means being able to imitate her in her spiritual maternity (which becomes spiritual paternity for men), a maternity or paternity which forms the people entrusted to them, not only in order to make them beautiful and holy, but to unite them with God and with one another.

This is the way Mary is mother. She is *Mater unitatis*.

Thus, we conclude: this point of our spirituality, "Mary," means that we live as she did, being in some way another Mary, who is the mother of unity.

The Holy Spirit

And now the Holy Spirit, the final point.

The third divine Person had not been explored in depth by our Church, at least not by the people. The Holy Spirit was said to be "the unknown God." We

---

49. Chiara Lubich, *Meditations*, p. 69; cf. *Christian Living Today*, p. 126.

knew that he existed. We prayed to him, *"Veni, Sancte Spiritus,"* but there was not much more.

In the Focolare Movement, the Holy Spirit is considered, above all, for what he is in God and for humankind.

He is the bond of unity between the divine Persons, Father and Son, and the bond of unity among Christians.

Moreover, because he can be present in the hearts of non-Christians of good will, he is in a certain way the bond of unity also with them.

One characteristic of the Focolare is that of listening to his voice within us. And that is not all, for we also learn to listen to the voice of him present among us, united in the risen Lord. Indeed, we attribute great importance to listening to the voice of the Spirit when Jesus is among us, because Jesus perfects our listening to his voice in each one of us. And here we can see the "something more" in our consideration of the Holy Spirit.

Because of this "something more" we have always experienced a special atmosphere in our gatherings, in our communities, in our model towns, in our small or large-scale meetings.

It is the effect of the presence of the risen Lord, who is among us and who brings with him the Holy Spirit.

The Holy Spirit, breath of Jesus and atmosphere of heaven, is also the breath of his body, the Church. And we are aware of his presence if the Church is itself in the full sense; that is, if it is kingdom of God, heaven come down on earth, because of unity.

These are the twelve points of our spirituality. Now it is up to all of us to live them with fullness, in order to make the Church, also through our Movement, ever more beautiful, harmonious, and strong and — with Mary, who is its model, its mother, its head, its queen — invincible.

Part 2

The Aspects

Introduction: Like a Rainbow

Through the charism of unity, the Lord wished to bring about in the Church not only a spirituality but also a society, which later was given the name Focolare Movement or Work of Mary.

Undoubtedly, this "Work" needs to have a soul (precisely what our communitarian spirituality is), but it also needs to have an order, a structure. And the Lord looked after this too.

If I remember correctly, it was in 1954. The spirituality appeared to be more or less complete. And one thing had become clear to us: we had to become another Jesus.

As early as 1946 we wrote in some notes: "Each of us must aim at being another Jesus as soon as possible. We must act as Jesus here on earth. We must put our human nature at God's disposal so that he can use it to make his beloved Son live again in us."[1]

But how could we do this? Baptism and the other sacraments had certainly already brought this about. But our adherence was necessary as well, and this could be summarized in one word: love. Love sums up the Christian law. If we love, we are another Jesus. And we are Jesus in all that we do. Our life, therefore, had to be love. If we had wanted

---

1. Chiara Lubich, Writing, "Unity," 2 December 1946, quoted in *A Call to Love* (Hyde Park, NY: New City Press, 1989), p. 29.

to describe what we should be, we would have had to say, "We are love," just as God is love. And if love was our life, love had to be our rule as well.

And here is an idea we had, perhaps an illumination.

Love is light, it is like a ray of light that passes through a drop of water and opens out to display a rainbow, whose seven colors we admire; they are all colors of light, which in turn display an infinite number of shades.

And just as the rainbow is red, orange, yellow, green, blue, indigo and violet, love, the life of Jesus in us, is manifested in different colors; it is expressed in various ways, each one different from the others.

Love, for example, leads to communion, it is communion. Jesus in us, because he is Love, brings about communion.

Love is not closed within itself but by its nature it spreads. Jesus in us, Love, reaches out to others in love.

Love elevates the soul. Jesus in us raises our souls to God. This is union with God, this is prayer.

Love heals. Jesus, Love in our hearts, is the health of our souls.

Love gathers people together in assembly. Jesus in us, because he is Love, joins our hearts.

Love is the source of wisdom. Jesus in us, Love, enlightens us.

Love gathers many into one, this is unity. Jesus in us fuses us into one.

These are the seven main expressions of love we had to live, and they represent an infinite number of expressions.

These seven expressions of love immediately appeared to us as the standard for our personal life, and they would also constitute the Rule of the Work of Mary as a whole, and later on of its various branches.

Because love is the principle of each of the above expressions, of each aspect (since it is always Jesus who lives in us in every aspect of life), our life would be marked by a wonderful unity.

Everything was to flow from love, be rooted in love; everything was to be an expression of the life of Jesus in us. And this would make human life attractive, fascinating. Consequently, our lives would not be dull and flat since they would not be made up of bits juxtaposed and disconnected (with the time for lunch, for example, having nothing to do with the moment for prayer, and with mission set aside only for a specific hour, and so on).

No. Now it would always be Jesus who prayed, Jesus who engaged in mission, Jesus who worked, Jesus who ate, Jesus who rested, and so on. Everything would be an expression of him.

The General Statutes of the Work of Mary and the Guidelines of its different branches[2] refer to these

---

2. The Focolare Movement or Work of Mary is composed of eighteen branches of which there are:
   — two sections of the Focolarini (men and women), which are the "supporting structure" of the Work of Mary.
   — ten branches (men and women Volunteers; Focolarini and Volunteer priests; Gens; men and women Religious; Gen boys and girls; Bishops friends of the Focolare).
   — six "movements" on a wider scale: New Families, New Humanity, Parish Movement, Diocesan Movement, Youth for a United World, Young for Unity.
   The General Statutes of the Work of Mary, approved on 29 June 1990 by a decree of the Pontifical Council of the Laity, established norms common for all the members. What characterizes each particular branch, on the other hand, is defined by the respective Guidelines, which are approved by the Movement's own General Assembly.

various expressions of love, that is, of the life of Jesus in us as our Rule, and as such they have been approved by the Church.

We would now like to begin re-examining the aspects of our life (its seven "colors," if we can say this) in order to see, among other things, if they too contain the "something more" that we discovered in the points of our spirituality, that is, if they are the expression of a life of communion.

Love is Communion

Since our Statutes apply to the entire Work of Mary with all its religious and lay vocations, the aspect of the *communion of goods* also includes our concept of *economy*, *work*, and *poverty*.

Communion of Goods

We know, of course, that others in the Church have lived and continue to live this communion, but for the most part they were, and still are, selected groups of persons, those with a special calling, such as monks and nuns in monasteries and convents.

In the Movement it is the whole of society that lives the communion of goods, including lay people, as it was among the first Christians. To reach this goal, we seek to mirror the communion of saints and we live according to the model of the Trinity, where it is true to say *Omnia mea tua sunt*, "all that is mine is yours" (cf. Jn 17:10).

There are those in the Focolare Movement who live out the communion of goods in a complete way. These are the celibate men and women Focolarini,[1] who give

---

1. "The focolare is, in the image of the family of Nazareth, a living together in the midst of the world of persons celibate and married, all totally committed, although in different ways, to God" (Chiara Lubich, *La dottrina spirituale*, p. 88).

to the Movement their entire salary and, by making a will, consign all their future capital and real estate to the poor, especially through the Focolare's formative, apostolic, and charitable activities.

Then there are others who give their surplus.

Saint Jerome says: "If you have more clothes and food than you need, you owe these to others." And before this Paul had said: "Not that others should have relief while you are burdened, but . . . that there may be equality" (2 Cor 8:13).

We have always lived the communion of goods in the Focolare, even from the very early days. I remember it started with a letter I wrote on the subject, which was read by the whole community, and which referred to the example of the first Christians.

The response was immediate and concrete. Month after month, we put into common everything we could: what was available and what we would need, and a record was kept of everything. We continued to do this throughout all of the Movement.

Later, when distinct sections, branches, and wide-ranging movements came about, each part practiced it within its own ranks. It is still like this.

The "something more" in this aspect lies in the way we deal with our goods and money. Usually, we do not give away our possessions or surplus as separate individuals, but we decide together what to give, and we put it in common beginning with the needy of our own branch.

Work

I would like to begin by saying that the prime source of income of our Movement is not work but the Providence of God that comes to us. It is always abundant and has covered as much as half of our financial needs.

In the Movement our constant experience is that if we seek the kingdom of God and his righteousness, all the rest comes as well (cf. Mt 6:33).

The second source of income is our *work*.

We give proper value to work in the Focolare, giving it great importance. This becomes evident also because most of our members are workers as, in the house of Nazareth, were Jesus, Mary, and Joseph.

Because loving makes us "another Jesus," we look at work the way he did. We consider our work:

— as an opportunity to do God's will, thus always being "turned toward the Father";

— as a very important occasion for finding fulfillment;

— as the possibility of being co-creators;

— as having the purpose of serving Jesus in the community;

— and, finally, as a chance to share what we earn with those in need.

Considering work in this way gives a higher meaning to life, and it is a constant source of joy.

Some religious orders, as we know, also underline the importance of work. Saint Benedict, for instance, had the motto: "*Ora et labora* (pray and work)."

What is the difference for us?

Many religious families do not always give to work all the above-mentioned meanings. At times work might seem to be a counterbalance to *prayer*, or simply something necessary to support oneself.

In his private life, however, Jesus was not so much a person who was *consecrated* to God, who withdrew to a monastery, as he was a worker. Therefore, the Focolare spirituality has a similar, if not identical, concept of work to the one Jesus had.

Given that at work we can be apprentices or experts, we have to specialize; we have to be familiar with the various rules of the workplace; we must endure the effort and fatigue our jobs demand; we need to be punctual; we have to take care of our earnings, administer our income, and so on.

To be a true worker, a member of the Focolare must look after all this and more. Love one's work, therefore.

DETACHMENT

At the same time, however, we must be detached from our work, because Christ requires detachment also from one's "fields." But here one of Jesus' promises comes true. Everyone who has left father, mother, wife, children or fields . . . will receive a hundred times more and will inherit eternal life (cf. Mt 19:29).

And because we strive to live like this, we receive the hundredfold, a capital that does not fall short.

This capital, the effect of God's Providence for our having put aside and given up everything for him, is what we have called *the capital of God*. In its regard, we found that we need to have three attitudes: to revitalize a spirit of poverty; not to live off interest; to determine that the Work of Mary cannot possess anything more than the goods it is actually putting to use.

Poverty

Closely connected to the aspects of the communion of goods, economy, and work, is poverty. We all strive to live it, and the consecrated members of our Movement even make a vow or promise of poverty.

The Guidelines of our different branches specify the various ways we practice poverty, which should be lived in the image of the poverty of Jesus, and which requires that goods be administered with openness and conform to specific rules.

Poverty within the Focolare is not an end in itself but an effect of love. Since we love, we give, and this makes us poor, having only what we need. But in the same way, poverty is also a *support* for love, an aid to love.

The Economy of Communion

The latest endeavor in this field is the *Economy of Communion*,[2] whose use of profits is intended to work together with the communion of goods. It aims at setting up businesses run by competent persons, who make them efficient and profitable. The profits are then put into common: one part to help the poor and give them what they need to live while they are unable to find work; another part to develop structures to educate persons animated by love; and a final part to develop the businesses themselves.

----

2. The idea of the Economy of Communion as a new way of doing business was proposed by Chiara Lubich in 1991 in Brazil, in response to the great poverty she saw in the *favelas,* the slums that circle the city of San Paolo, and which Cardinal Arns, its archbishop, called a "crown of thorns."

We found what God told Catherine of Siena, in her *Dialogue*, concerning clerics who did not pay much attention to such matters: "with regard to temporal goods, I told you that they should be distributed in three portions: one for their own needs [this makes us think of the profits that are used for the businesses]; one for the poor; and one for the use of the Church [which could indicate the structures of a Movement that has the nature of Church]."[3]

This perhaps serves as a confirmation for us.

---

3. Catherine of Siena, *The Dialogue* (New York: Paulist Press, 1980), n. 121, p. 232.

Love Radiates

Outreach or, as it is more commonly called in some circles, apostolic activities.

The subject is vast. We will limit ourselves to gathering early ideas here and there from the writings of the early years. Reading through just a few pages on this aspect is enough to make us understand that what John Paul II said of our spirituality holds true also for our apostolic activities: "The first inspiring spark was love."[1]

Yes, it was love; a spark was enkindled; it spread light all around and burst into flames.

Love reaches out; love *itself* bears witness.

I know that in other environments it is said that, "Love is the soul of the apostolate." But it is much more. Love is the *first* form of apostolate, love of our neighbor as an expression of our love for God.

Each member of the Work of Mary is not called only to evangelize along the lines of "Go therefore and make disciples of all nations . . ." (Mt 28:19). When the word enters into our actions, it should not be only an exposition of the Catholic faith. It has to be undergirded by witness (the witness of love) and its meaning filled out by experience. This is the way it was with the first Christians, and this is the way it is now.

---

1. *Insegnamenti di Giovanni Paolo II* VII/2, pp. 223–225.

Love, not Proselytism

A letter from 1948 helps us to see two things: how love is the driving force of outreach and how outreach is essential to the Christian life.

I wrote to some young people:

"May the whole city fall into the furnace of the Love of the Heart of Jesus.

"My sisters, Jesus rejoices to know that other sisters have joined you, but at the same time, he weeps because you have conquered few people to his Heart.

"Forgive me for saying this to you! I should first reproach myself, but let me tell you what I think.

"Don't tell me that they (your fellow citizens) are hard to convince, etc., etc.

"It's not true. *Love conquers all!*

"It is love that is lacking in our hearts! Too often we believe that loving God means (only) going to religious meetings, praying a long time, doing hours of adoration.

"Religion is not only this! . . .

"It is (also) looking for the lost sheep, making ourselves all things to all people! It is loving in a practical, gentle, and strong way all the persons around us as we love ourselves, and wishing for them what we wish for ourselves. . . .

"The Lord urgently needs souls like this: souls on fire. . . .

"And how few he finds . . .

"Let's love. . . . Let's widen the circle of unity to include the greatest number of souls possible.

"*This* is love of God!"[2]

---

2. Chiara Lubich, Unpublished Letter, Trent, 4 November 1948.

In 1954, after having concentrated for a while on setting down the essential structure of the Focolare (withdrawing in the meantime a little from apostolic activities), this is what I wrote:

"The hour is coming in which we must rekindle our Ideal in the world . . . like a fire.

"For this to happen, however, we must return to the fruitful life we had in the early days when we won over very many people to God simply because we wanted to express our love to the Lord.

"This lack of self-interest was like a magnet that attracted many, and the community grew up around us.

"Do you remember?"[3]

In 1956 we were already in correspondence with people in other nations where the Focolare was taking its first steps.

This letter is addressed to a group in France:

"Dearest friends in France, I read your letters and shared your happiness for the day-meeting that was held in Grenoble.

"[Our people] returned full of joy. . . . They told me that it was like re-living the early days of our Ideal when the first Focolarine lived in Piazza Cappuccini.

"This made me immensely happy. I thought, if ten years ago there was hardly anything in Italy, only a great 'fire' burning in Trent, and now Italy is (here and there) sowed with the Ideal . . . in a few years (the same thing will happen) in . . . France. . . .

"I'm sure of this, because the strength of our Movement is not you but Jesus among you, and he does great things.

---

3. Chiara Lubich, Unpublished Letter, Rome, 3 November 1954.

"But Jesus, of course, uses you.

"And so I beg you with all my heart, love him madly! . . .

"France must fall into the net of Jesus. God wants it: may his kingdom come, come, come!

"You are small, poor, beset with problems. But for this very reason God will work. This is what he did with us; this is what he will do with you."[4]

Love Anchored in Suffering

To spread our Ideal more effectively, we counted very much on suffering.

"Dear friend, I was very happy with your letter. It reflected the soul of someone whom Jesus has called to follow him in his forsakenness.

"Take advantage of the solitude he has left you in, so that you can be alone with him alone. But then go at once to carry out his will, which is to bring fire into the world. . . .

"If you are on the cross, you will draw everyone to you . . . to Jesus. . . ."[5]

We recommended prayer and mortification as means for reaching our goal (which proves that ours is both a collective and personal spirituality).

"Dear people responsible for zones,[6] at the Center of the Movement we have decided that you should visit your entire zone personally, bringing to each soul the fire of God's love. . . .

---

4. Chiara Lubich, Unpublished Letter, Rome, 13 December 1956.
5. Cf. Chiara Lubich, Unpublished Letter, Rome, 22 April 1955.
6. "People responsible for zones" are persons who coordinate the life of the Focolare Movement in its various territories throughout the world, which are called "zones."

"While you do this work, be ardent in prayer and union with God, so that this very delicate task may be carried out in depth and with excellent results, and so that people will give their best for the glory of God.

"Keep yourselves mortified and far from the world around you. We will never know so well what is happening, and we have to know it, as when we are united to God alone and completely lost in our Ideal."[7]

The fire that Jesus brought is love, and love conquers. The following passage is from 1955:

" 'I came to bring fire to the earth . . .' (Lk 12:49). Why fire? Because he is fire; because Christ is God and God is love!

"[But] fire burns when it consumes something, when it conquers. A love that does not conquer, dies out! Therefore, we cannot fool ourselves thinking that we have Christ within us if this fire doesn't burn, if this fire doesn't conquer."[8]

Apostolate Carried Out in Unity

The typical way for the Focolare to do its apostolic activity is above all to do it in unity: "May they all be one, so that the world may believe" (cf. Jn 17:21).

And the "something more" of our outreach, or, if you like, our apostolic activity, lies in this unity, which is necessary and obligatory for those who live this spirituality. We can say that it is "something more," because this is not generally required of those who want to do apostolic work.

7. Cf. Chiara Lubich, Unpublished Letter, Rome, 16 June 1955.
8. Cf. Chiara Lubich, Unpublished Talk, "The Seven Colors," Vigo di Fassa (Italy), 19 August 1955.

Another writing says, "Identifying with Jesus, being another Jesus. . . . We must be so for all those around us, with no exceptions. . . . Then, as soon as this spirit of ours touches someone's soul, we should remain linked spiritually to him or her so that Jesus may live among us, and that in him we may find the strength to conquer other souls to the perfect love of God."[9]

The following episode has always remained fixed in the depth of our hearts. In it lies the secret of our outreach, its necessary departure point. It is in a talk from 1962:

"As I was walking along the streets of Einsiedeln, in Switzerland, I saw many people of various religious orders passing by. The different habits of the sisters and priests were very beautiful against the background of such a splendid natural setting. I understood there that the founders were really inspired in dressing their followers in that particular way.

"[Among these], I was particularly impressed by Charles de Foucauld's Little Sisters of Jesus. They rode by on their bicycles, with very lively faces and peasant scarves on their heads. Their expressive faces reminded me of their founder, de Foucauld, who, they say, cried out the gospel with the whole style of his life.

"In fact, those sisters seemed to say: 'Blessed are the poor in spirit, blessed are they who mourn, blessed . . .'

"These are not the beatitudes that the world would like to have but the scandal of the gospel.

"Then, I too felt a great desire to be able to give my witness, also in an external way.

"[But] . . . no solution came to me.

---

9. Cf. Chiara Lubich, Unpublished Letter, Ostia (Italy), 18 April 1950.

"At a certain point I said to one of my companions: 'You know . . . I saw how those sisters had an effect on me not through their words but by the way they dressed . . .' and I said I wished we could do the same. But how could *we* tell people about God? 'Ah,' I said, 'By this everyone will know that you are my disciples, if you have love for one another' (Jn 13:35).

"Mutual love, therefore, was to be our distinctive sign. Dying to ourselves in mutual love is our (typical) apostolic activity."[10]

Then if we use the spoken word as well (and "woe betide me if I do not proclaim the gospel!" 1 Cor 9:16), if throughout the years we have felt the urgency and, I would say, the calling to proclaim it even from the housetops, if we give talks and repeat them for the good of many, using modern means of communication, all this should come afterwards.

"Structures" Evangelize Too

However, witness and outreach are the duty not only of *persons* who are united but also of structures, beginning with the focolare. From this outreach, then, the focolare itself acquires new meaning.

In a writing from 1950, we read, "The focolare is made up of people who live a life in common solely in order to realize among themselves and around them the testament of Jesus, 'Father, may they all be one.'

---

10. Cf. Chiara Lubich, Unpublished Talk to the Focolarine, "The First Two Aspects of Our Spirituality," Grottaferrata (Rome), 25 December 1962.

"Through their mutual love . . . they are transformed into Jesus, into love, and their focolare truly becomes Fire, all Fire.[11]

"Thus if someone visits the focolare . . . and is not inflamed to the point that he or she goes away lit up, ablaze and in peace just as the Focolarini are, then the fire in that focolare has gone out.

"[And] a cold focolare does harm, it's not that it does nothing, it actually does harm. Whereas a focolare that is ablaze does what it should: it does good."[12]

Therefore, the focolare is a powerful means of outreach.

And this holds true today for all our forms of community: from the nuclei of the Volunteers to Gen units, from our headquarters to our little towns, from clergy houses to convents to environmental cells, and so on.[13]

In 1956 another part of our structure, a temporary one, was taking place: one of our Mariapolises[14] in the Dolomite mountains of the Alps. It was a jewel, a divine diamond, a heavenly means of outreach. But it was also a place to strengthen oneself spiritually, so as to continue one's apostolic witness to others.

As we read in something written at that time, we can already foresee a Mariapolis that was to be permanent:

---

11. There is an underlying wordplay in the Italian. The word "Focolare" means hearth or fireplace and comes from the same root as the "fuoco" which means fire. For a focolare to be on fire is to say that the fireplace is ablaze.
12. Cf. Chiara Lubich, Unpublished Writing, "The Focolare," 1950.
13. The reference is to different types of groupings within the various branches of the Work of Mary.
14. See note 16, p. 141.

"Many have spoken of the Mariapolis and they've spoken well of it. It's logical, because the City of Mary . . . could not help but have a special fascination and, at times, extraordinary effects.

"Catherine of Siena, however, says that you know something well by studying it, but even better by studying its opposite."[15]

This is what I wrote, "When most of the citizens of the Mariapolis had left . . . everything up there seemed to have ended. There was still that blue sky, those green meadows, those majestic Saint Martin mountain slopes, those pathways, that church: everything was still beautiful, yes, but *Mary* was missing; her city, her family was missing. A family made up of all kinds of children . . . of people who were very united to God — some who had always lived an innocent life, others who had just returned beneath the gaze of the Mother, long-awaited, now happy like all the others.

"I assure you that ever since I came to know our Ideal, I tried never to look back in life, but those empty roads, that sun-filled valley, now had the appearance of a corpse and made me think again of those two enchanting months filled with the presence of Mary. Perhaps more than looking back I was looking up and, without realizing it, I was asking Mary to perpetuate this city of hers here on earth.

"Certainly, we must make every city another Mariapolis, yet (it may be that the Lord wants) a place to give continual glory to Mary through an ever-enkindled life of the Ideal. It would be a place where one can take refuge and be renewed like a soldier returning

---

15. Cf. Chiara Lubich, Unpublished Letter, 22 September 1956.

home from the barracks, a foretaste of heaven while still on earth in the Church militant, a place to acquire new strength and return to battle so that the kingdom of God and his Church may advance in the world: a permanent Mariapolis.

"May Our Lady grant us this gift."[16]

A foretaste of heaven. . . . Perhaps it is true; the permanent Mariapolis of Loppiano has been described as a "videoclip" of paradise.[17]

Now Mary has already built, or is in the process of building, about twenty of these videoclips of paradise.

16. Cf. Chiara Lubich, Unpublished Letter, 22 September 1956.
17. Loppiano, the first of the Focolare's model towns, located near Florence, Italy. Founded in 1965, today it has more than 800 inhabitants. See note 16, p. 141.

Love Uplifts

The third aspect of the spirituality of unity is the one that concerns our spiritual life.

Love within us, which makes us another Jesus, not only creates "communion," not only "reaches out," but it also "uplifts." It is the principle and source of our inner life, of our union with God, of our true prayer. In this talk we will focus upon prayer, meditation, and union with God.

Prayer

With regard to prayer, this time too we will refer to writings and talks that we have preserved from past years, in order to look more closely at how the Holy Spirit, through the charism of unity, taught us to pray.

We will not go beyond this to look at the communitarian prayer offered by the liturgy, nor will we speak of prayer in the lives of people with particular vocations, such as priests and religious. We will, rather, examine prayer as required of everyone in general.

Prayer, as we know, is our relationship with God. It is a building block of our very being, of our being human. Indeed, since we are created in the image and likeness of God, we are capable of a direct, personal relationship with God; we are persons who can address God as "you."

That humans have a natural disposition to pray becomes clear when we come to know our brothers and sisters of other religions. We find they have prayer texts which are amazingly beautiful. They bear witness to the secret, but effective, action of God who always urges people to pray.

HUMAN BEINGS ARE TRULY HUMAN IF THEY PRAY

And the same applies to us Christians. We are brothers and sisters of Jesus, through grace; and in him we find the model of how to relate to the Father. Jesus, in fact, did not only preach, work miracles, and call the disciples to follow him; he also immersed himself in prayer. Indeed, just as Jesus was always in communion with his Father, always in his presence, so it should be with his followers.

We all know that Christians pray in different ways. It is possible, therefore, to highlight the main and typical ways of praying among those who have been given the charism of unity.

These characteristics clearly emerge if we compare our prayer life with that of Christians, even the ones who knew their Christianity best, at least those in our countries, at the time when the Focolare began.

I remember that in speaking of prayer we said that "one needs to put to work the mind, the will and the heart. Our mind helps us reflect on the words we hear; our will leads us to formulate resolutions on the basis of our reflections; our heart draws us to love what we have promised to do."[1]

These were certainly excellent suggestions.

---

1. From an unpublished letter of Silvia Lubich, Bozzana (Italy), 22 July 1939. (Silvia, the author's baptismal name, was changed to Chiara during her time in the Franciscan Third Order.)

Nonetheless, within the Focolare Movement, prayer immediately became something else. From the early months we emphasized, for instance, the duty to "pray always," as Jesus requested. But how could we pray always? We knew that we couldn't do this by multiplying the prayers we said.

We could pray always by being Jesus. Jesus, in fact, prays always. If in performing any action it was not we who lived but Christ living in us, through love, our day would become a continuous prayer. And this would be possible if we based our life on love, being a living expression of the word "love," which sums up all the Law and the Prophets.

Another way to "pray always" — which we practiced a little later — was to offer to God during the day one action after the other by saying short expressions of love, such as: "For you Jesus."

Thus all our actions were transformed into sacred actions. We were convinced then, as we are now, that by offering our daily work to God in this way, and performing it well, we cooperate with him in the creation of the world; we are co-creators with him.

And this way of praying is very much in tune with our times. Today we see the world and the whole universe in evolution, and human beings are reminded of their duty to "subdue the earth" (cf. Gn 1:28).

In addition, when we work for a Work of God and, therefore, for the Church, we participate with Christ in the redemption of the world.

The extensive activity that has always characterized the Focolare could have compromised prayer, making it imperfect and unworthy of being offered to God. This is why we always stressed that we needed to give prayer a privileged place in our lives.

Already during the early times, we wrote, "What importance does it have to be so committed to bringing many people to God when our own souls remain small and imperfect because we do not find a really peaceful time for our own nourishment in prayer?

"What importance does all this have, when the very prayers we have sacred duty to say are said in the midst of countless distractions and recited only superficially, hurriedly, or are shortened in length?"[2]

OBSTACLES TO PRAYER

With regard to the failings we could have in our prayer life, I wrote:

"We have the possibility of living in communion with the All-Powerful God and yet we do it so seldom, in such a hurry, and often reluctantly. At the end of our lives we will regret having given so little time to prayer."[3]

Another obstacle to prayer could be a state of spiritual aridity. In those who are committed to living the spirituality of unity, however, we note a certain facility in overcoming aridity in prayer. This too is nothing other than an aspect of Jesus Forsaken, one of his faces, and just as we know how to pass from the cross to the resurrection in other circumstances, we ought to do so here.

It seems to us to be very providential that we can, generally, overcome aridity. Since most of us live in the

---

2. Chiara Lubich, *On the Holy Journey* (Hyde Park, NY: New City Press, 1988), p. 35.
3. Chiara Lubich, *Fragments of Wisdom* (Mumbai, India: St. Paul Press, 1991), p. 77.

midst of the world, it is important that certain spiritual trials are not drawn out. We have other temptations to conquer.

We feel that one's physical condition is important for prayer, too. In fact, we try not to overtire ourselves prior to these moments so as not to come before God without any strength or with little ability to concentrate, and be forced to give God the least productive moments of our day.

PREPARATION FOR PRAYER

We are also convinced that we should prepare for prayer. The experts say that prayer needs a remote and an immediate preparation.

The remote preparation is to keep our hearts free of any attachment. It seems to me that all the members of the Movement are actively committed to this kind of preparation. In fact, our entire life is constantly focused on loving Jesus crucified and forsaken; and that we lose, we put everything else to one side.

Often we speak of "cutting," of "pruning," and above all of the detachment required in being outside ourselves in an attitude of loving others, in living the "other" and not ourselves. Yes, we hope that this preparation is present in our lives. At least it is what we strive for every day.

The immediate preparation, instead, consists in always starting with a moment of recollection.

We became aware, and are still aware, of the absolute necessity and value of prayer.

"In heaven," I wrote in 1989, "where we hope to go, life will not consist of carrying out apostolic endeavors. It will consist of praising, thanking, and adoring God, the Most Holy Trinity. We must learn now to live as we will then."[4]

How Jesus Prayed

But there is a prayer in the Focolare Movement that, with the infinite and divine riches it contains, is all enclosed in one word, just one word, which Jesus said and taught us, and which the Spirit puts on our lips.

Jesus prayed, he prayed to his Father. For him the Father was "Abba," which means dad or papa, the one he turned to with infinite trust and boundless love. He prayed to him from within the heart of the Trinity, where he is the Second Divine Person.

Since he came on earth out of love for us, however, it was not enough for him to be the only one in this privileged position of prayer. By dying for us, redeeming us, he made us children of God, as he is, his own brothers and sisters. And through the Holy Spirit he gave us too the possibility of being introduced into the heart of the Trinity, in him, together with him, by means of him, so that we too have the possibility of repeating the same divine invocation: "Abba, Father!" (Mk 14:36; Rm 8:15). "Dad, my Dad, our Dad," with all that this means: total surrender to his love, certainty in his protection, security, divine consolation, strength, ardor born in the hearts of those who are certain of being loved. . . .

This is Christian prayer, an extraordinary type of prayer. One does not find it anywhere else, nor in other religions. The most someone who believes in a Divine Being does is to implore, venerate and adore, while

---

4. Chiara Lubich, *On the Holy Journey*, pp. 83–84.

remaining, so to speak, "outside" of the Divine Being. Here we enter into the very heart of God.

Naturally, we can say "Abba, Father!" with all that this word implies only if the Spirit speaks it in us.

And again, for this to happen, we need — as required by the charism of unity — to be Jesus, nothing but Jesus.

Meditation

The prayer life of a member of the Movement also includes meditation.

It is logical that, if we are called to a spirituality that is both personal and collective, we need to build up along with the "exterior castle" (that is, the Focolare Movement, the Church), the "interior castle," that is, the union of our soul with God within us. And this is achieved especially through meditation.

A preparation is necessary for this too. If we do not make even the slightest effort to recollect ourselves and "close the shutters," so to speak, or, in other words "turn off our senses" (close our eyes, for example), so as to seek him, then God cannot let himself be found (the mystics say that God is at the center of our soul) and he cannot spend time with us, flooding us with his presence, giving us all the beautiful things he brings.

We found this writing from 1972:

> The Trinity inside of me!
> The abyss inside of me!
> The vastness inside of me!
> The boundless love inside of me!
> The Father

Jesus proclaimed to us
        inside of me!
The Word!
The Holy Spirit,
who I want to have always
to serve the Work of Mary,
inside of me!
I ask nothing more.
I want to dwell in this abyss,
        to lose myself in this sun,
to live together with Everlasting Life.
What then?
Prune away the life outside
and live what is inside:
The more I cut off communication
with the outside
(words that are often unnecessary, etc),
the more I converse with the Trinity
inside of me."[5]

WHAT SHOULD WE USE FOR MEDITATION?

We have always been convinced that we should meditate for the most part on Holy Scripture and on writings to do with our spirituality. This is the suggestion given to those who belong to an ecclesial Movement. It is very helpful when we wake up to start the day by meditating, for example, on the passages chosen for the scripture readings of the day. Afterwards, we share more deeply in the Liturgy, and it becomes a much more satisfying and beautiful experience.

---

5. Chiara Lubich, Diary, 22 May 1972, in *La dottrina spirituale*, pp. 192–193.

If we want to read spiritual texts, biographies and writings of saints or something else, we can do so, and it is an excellent idea, but as spiritual reading.

AND HOW SHOULD WE MEDITATE?

To meditate we begin by sitting calmly and reading a book, after having put ourselves in the presence of God. If, at some point, we have the impression that he takes the soul and uplifts it, then we must close the book, stay with him, listen to him, answer him, love him, adore him, ask him for graces.

After a while, we may feel that the conversation can be considered complete. Then we open the book again and continue reading. In practice, meditation should become a true conversation with God. We feel listened to, we speak to him, and our whole soul is taken up by him. It is like opening a bottle of perfume whose fragrance permeates the whole day.

Our experience shows that it is not good to meditate with an "ulterior motive," that is, taking notes that may be useful to other people. This can be done later. During meditation it is best to be alone with God. Nor should we go on and on reading, giving in to spiritual greed. This would not be love.

THE EFFECTS OF MEDITATION

If meditation is done well, it often has the following effect. It makes us lose interest in the things of this world, even beautiful things, because it takes us to another reality experienced in the depths of our hearts: God, his love, union with him. We then go back among the people and the things of this world with our intentions all permeated with the supernatural.

Union with God

First of all, we have always been convinced that the charism of unity must bring people to a great union with God, precisely because of the "charism of unity."

This is how something I wrote speaks of our union with God:

"Unity is the word that summarizes our entire spirituality: unity with God, unity with our neighbors. And more specifically, our typical way is unity with our neighbor in order to attain union with God.

"In fact, the Holy Spirit revealed to us a way that is distinctly ours and fully evangelical, a way to unite us to God. Generally speaking we do not seek God first of all in the depths of our hearts where he dwells, or in nature. We look for him and we find him by going through our neighbor, loving our neighbor.

"Only in this way — by loving our brothers and sisters — are we guaranteed unity with him as well, for then we find him alive and beating in our hearts. In turn, unity with God leads us to go out to our fellow human beings; it helps us to make our love for them something that is not false, nor insufficient, nor superficial, but rather true, full, complete, verified by sacrifice; it includes the readiness to give one's life, and is capable of achieving unity."[6]

This is a common experience ever since the Focolare was born. After having loved our neighbors during the course of the day, when evening comes we find in our hearts union with God. This union was blessed and

---

6. Chiara Lubich, *Cercando le cose di lassù* (Rome: Città Nuova, 1992), p. 156.

greatly blessed especially by those members of our Movement who live in the midst of the world. This "experiencing" God, his kingdom in us, is the most important antidote to the materialism that reigns everywhere and influences so many.

The following writing is a prayer from many years ago that underscores the truth that we find God by loving our brothers and sisters.

"When unity with our brothers and sisters is complete, when it has flowered anew and more fully from difficulties, then, as night fades into day and tears into light, often, I find you. Lord. Going back into the temple of my soul, I meet you; or as soon as circumstances leave me alone, you invite me, you draw me, gently but firmly, into your divine presence.

"Then you alone rule within me and outside me. . . . The soul is immersed as if in some delicious nectar and the heart seems to have become the chalice that contains it. The soul is all a silent song known only to you: a melody that reaches you because it comes from you and is made of you. . . .

"And . . . strangely — strange to the human way of thinking — we have gone out to our brothers and sisters all day long and, in the evening, we have found the Lord, who has dissolved every trace, every memory of creatures."[7]

And we feel that this way is particularly pleasing to the Lord. We can observe, moreover, that for those who go to God following a way that is more individual in nature, the loving and spontaneous dialogue with him

---

7. Chiara Lubich, *Meditations,* pp. 109–110; cf. also *Christian Living Today,* p. 147.

requires a struggle, at times painful one, that takes time; it is a conquest and not always successful.

Instead, for those who journey along a more collective way, like ours, we can affirm that this dialogue is perceived, at least in certain moments, from the beginning. And even children can experience it.

Moreover, it has been our experience that this union with God can reach the point, in time, of being the underpinning of our every action, the foundation of our being.

And what happens after we have experienced union with God?

"Union with God," we affirmed on another occasion, "is developed by means of many graces God gives to our souls. Paul, listing the graces given to him, speaks even of revelations. For us, there might have been certain movements, divine impulses to our wills, urging us to renew our conversion over and over again. It can happen at our meetings, through a strong presence of Jesus in our midst. Or there might be certain consolations or illuminations or other gifts."[8]

Very many of us, certainly, have made an effort to love our neighbor and have overcome trials and received graces. The little plant of our union with God should be present and have grown in our souls, and each could tell us its story. We could also list its fruits.

All this is a very important and delicate spiritual heritage, which we can perceive only with the senses of our souls. For those living in the midst of the world, this heritage is something out of the ordinary, something miraculous. It is the kingdom of God within us.

---

8. Chiara Lubich, *Journey to Heaven*, p. 46.

What we need to do is to not waste it but guard and look after it, reminding ourselves that it is part of the life we will experience when we will leave this world. . . .

And we can guard and look after it, helping this spiritual heritage to grow by working on four fronts: striving always to be in an attitude of love for our brothers and sisters; overcoming every trial, great or small, through love for Jesus forsaken; reminding ourselves, with gratitude, of the graces God has generously given to us in life; and, finally, since we are talking about our inner life, our relationship with God, we should add fuel to the fire by taking care of our prayer life in a special way: morning and evening prayers, meditation, participation in the eucharist, and so forth.

We should be convinced, as experts in the spiritual life affirm, that God calls everyone to this union.

Furthermore, so as to give the proper place to prayer, in the Work of Mary we always have before us Mary, the Mother of Jesus. How do we imagine Mary, how is she described to us in the scriptures? How has she been depicted in paintings, songs, and statues by artists throughout the ages?

Surely not as an unrecollected person, as someone who is restless, who is impetuous, always rushing, mindful only of external things. No, we think of her as a person who, filled with mystical beauty, discloses an immense treasure hidden in her heart: God.

And so it should be for us, too.

Love Heals

Our previous subject was a reflection on our spiritual life and, to be more precise, on the spiritual life of each one of us personally.

Now we would like to think over the fourth aspect, a further effect of the love we seek to live out. It is the one concerning not so much the life of our soul but, rather, of our body.

The fourth aspect is about physical life, health, the whole course of human existence, including illness and death, as well as resurrection; and it is also about creation, which human beings sum up in themselves.

And because the vocation of the entire Work of Mary is love, we live all moments of human existence, in this life and the next, by loving and as expressions of love.

In this brief discussion I will be able to give only a basic knowledge of these aspects, as we understand them and as we seek to live them among ourselves. As always, I will draw from suggestions, ideas, highlights, thoughts, and illuminations that we have received down through the years, from the beginning.

What importance do we Christians usually give to the body?

Paul VI tells us: "The human body . . . is sacred. . . . Yes, it is the dwelling place of the divine. . . . Human life is imbued with the thought of God. Man is his image.

Furthermore, when grace sanctifies a person, his or her body becomes not only the instrument or organ of the soul, but also the mysterious temple of the Holy Spirit. . . . It is like saying," continues Paul VI, "that a new conception of the human body is opening up before our eyes; . . . which in no way alters the vision of the physical and biological reality. On the contrary, it enlightens it. It enhances it with a new appeal . . . which surpasses the appeal of the senses and aesthetics, which are so real and strong, and many times, so wicked and fatal. It is an appeal which we could call mystical, a new appeal which neither pleasure nor beauty suggest, but which the love of Christ inspires."[1]

On Health

If the body is to be considered in this way, how should we behave toward it?

Let us first give some thought to our health.

In our present-day society, as was also true in the past, there is sometimes an excessive concern for the human physique. In a frantic concern to satisfy current standards of beauty, for example, people are sometimes advised to adopt mistaken dietary behaviors, which can bring about serious illnesses.

But we, committed Christians, how do we treat the body? We can note in general an all-too-common defect, namely, that people are often caught up in activism even on those days meant for rest. Often, health takes second place.

---

1. *Insegnamenti di Paolo VI,* I, p. 141.

Not giving the needed care to the body necessarily leads to a lack of balance between what is consumed by the mind and soul, and what is given to the body.

There is some consolation, although no justification, in the fact that the saints themselves — I am thinking of Saint Ignatius — ruined their health, even though it served as a lesson to them for regulating the life of their followers.

Thoughts like these have often been the object of concern for us members of the Focolare. That is why every now and then we have to advise that our vacations really be vacations. We should organize the days by filling them — so as not to have the temptation to work — with whatever is good for our health. We must forget our usual commitments and go walking in the mountains or swimming in the sea, playing sports or rowing on a lake; playing open-air games or, in the evening, games around the table; watching wholesome documentaries or relaxing films. . . .

Everything should be well ordered, with plenty of sleep, without too rigid a timetable. There should be relaxation each day, and we should eat well.

And in all of this we need to maintain and improve our relationship with God, so as to hear his voice clearly, which asks us to look after our bodies for as long as he wills, ready to offer them to him when his call comes.[2]

But more than anything else what is beneficial to our health is a well-ordered life, day in, day out. Many saints, whom we can take as our models, have been of this opinion. In the Rule of the Congregation of Saint Joseph, founded by Saint Leonardo Murialdo, we find

---

2. Cf. Chiara Lubich, Diary of 4 August 1968.

written: "The serenity of community life is favored . . .
by a wise, well-ordered plan, which ensures each brother
time for prayer, work, study, and rest."[3]

We for our part have the same possibility if we want it.

On Illness

And when our health fails, when we fall sick?

In Eastern and African cultures, sickness is often
interpreted in a religious way, as a religious reawak-
ening, for example. Western society, which is based
above all on scientific and technological progress and, as
a consequence, is characterized by the frantic pursuit of
a better life, usually loses the spiritual-human signifi-
cance of illness and interprets it as the awkward weak-
ness of an organism, which breaks down for various
reasons and which medical science then cures, or hopes
to cure in the very near future.

Today's medicine, with a few exceptions, is based in
its anthropological principles on a certain dualism: it
looks upon the body, with its organs and mechanisms,
as though it were something detached from that marvel-
lous holistic reality that is the human being.

And what do we think about all this in our Movement?

We have clear convictions concerning sick persons.

When someone is not well, we must seek every way
and means to restore him or her to good health, because
the health of its members is not theirs alone but is the
heritage of the Focolare.

---

3. *Regola*, Direttorio, #15 (Rome, 1984).

At the same time, those who are ill are asked to be detached from their health. But not only this. They are encouraged to see even illness and death as gifts of God, because they are expressions of his will and therefore of his love. At the first signs of any illness, we are invited to believe and to say that everything is love, the love of God, recalling Therese of Lisieux, who did not focus on her infirmity when she first spat up blood; rather, she said: "My Spouse has arrived."[4]

If illness and death are expressions of God's love, what special meaning do they have?

In our view, illnesses are means in the hands of God's providence, in order to carve out from the shapeless bulk of our egos, the figure of Jesus, Jesus himself.

We have always been attracted, therefore, by the explanation that Vincent de Paul gives of illness. "What happens to us," he says, "is like what happens to a block of marble from which one wants to carve out a beautiful statue of the Virgin. What will the sculptor have to do in order to put the idea he has in mind into a form? He will have to take hold of a hammer and remove from the block all that is superfluous. And so he begins to hit the top of the block with well-directed blows . . . ; in fact, it looks as though he wants to smash it to pieces. But after he has removed the larger parts of the block, he uses a smaller hammer and then a chisel to begin shaping the figure in all its finest details. Finally, he uses ever more delicate instruments to give the statue that refined perfection he has in mind.

---

4. Cf. Therese of Lisieux, *Story of a Soul*, transl. John Clarke, O.C.D. (Washington, D.C.: ICS Publications, 1996), p. 211.

"God uses the same technique with us. Take the case of a Daughter of Charity or a missionary. Before God draws them from the world, their lives appear to be coarse, unrefined, and brutal, like large blocks of marble. But God wants to turn them into beautiful statues and so he begins to work on them and to strike them from above with strong hammer blows. . . .

"Whoever sees outward appearances alone (in spiritual or physical trials) might be inclined to say that this Daughter is unfortunate. But if one discerns God's plan, he will see that all these blows were dealt for the sole purpose of giving form to that beautiful idea."[5]

In the Focolare we also have our own view of illness and of those who are sick.

In another diary from April 1968 we find:

"In our work, in the triumphs . . . brought about by this vigorous and flourishing Movement, at times we are tempted to see people who are suffering as marginal cases to be looked after, to be visited, but to be helped if we can so that they may soon resume their activity, as if such activity were our primary duty, the center of our life.

"But this is not so. Those among us who are suffering, who are lying ill, who are dying, are the chosen ones. They are at the center of the hierarchy of love in the Movement. They are the ones who do the most, who achieve the most."[6]

And at another time we wrote: "Those who are ill should be seen as living hosts who unite their suffering

---

5. M. Auclair, *La parola a San Vincenzo dè Paoli* (Rome, 1971), pp. 289–290.
6. Chiara Lubich, Unpublished Diary of 11 April 1968.

to that of Christ, thus giving the best contribution to the development of the Work of Mary and of the Church."[7]

Pope John XXIII was of the same opinion. He wrote to a bishop who had retired: "Now your task has changed (in relation to the Church): you must pray for her. And this is no less important than action for her."

It would be beautiful and interesting at this point to examine some rules of life of other religious families in order to see how consistent the Holy Spirit is in suggesting to various founders norms similar to our own.

In the Rule of Benedict, for example, we read in chapter 36: "First and foremost, care must be given to the sick. . . ."[8]

In an early rule of Saint Francis we find: "I beg the sick brother to thank God for everything and to desire to be whatever the Lord wills, whether sick or well, because God teaches all those He has destined for eternal life . . . as the Lord says: 'Those whom I love, I correct and chastise' (Rev 3:19)."[9]

Illness, therefore, is love. For Francis as for us, all that makes us suffer is love.

Moreover, we see illnesses, with their burden of suffering, as trials from God for the final trial: our passage to the next life.

We wrote in the sixties:

"God, in becoming man, and therefore in being mortal, was born on this earth to die.

---

7. General Statutes of the Work of Mary, art. 52.
8. G. Turbessi (ed.), *Regole monastiche antiche* (Rome, 1978), p. 442.
9. *The Saint*, Francis of Assisi: Early Documents, pp. 71–72.

"This is the meaning of life: to live like the grain of wheat — whose destiny it is to die and decay — in preparation for the true life of eternity. . . .

"We have to see all the illnesses that befall us as steps prepared by the love of God to help us scale the heights, as trials to prepare us for *the* trial. We are like small hosts, not yet completely consumed, but awaiting that moment which will come for all of us, the full '*consummatum est*' (Jn 19:30).

"And so: mortals with the Mortal One, in order to rise with him and to begin a Life that will never end.

"Lord, may the doing of your will be incense that we offer in this 'mass' we are preparing."[10]

And the writing entitled: "His mass and ours" is well known. It speaks of suffering. It may be useful here to quote a part of it because it contains the meaning that illness and suffering have for us:

> If you suffer and your suffering is such
> that it prevents any activity,
> remember the mass.
> Jesus in the mass,
> today as once before,
> does not work, does not preach:
> Jesus sacrifices himself out of love.
> In life
> we can do many things, say many words,
> but the voice of suffering,
> maybe unheard and unknown to others,
> is the most powerful word,
> the one that pierces heaven.

---

10. Cf. Chiara Lubich, *Fragments of Wisdom*, pp. 43–44 (translation revised).

If you suffer,
immerse your pain in his:
say your mass;
and if the world does not understand
do not worry
all that matters
is that you are understood by Jesus, Mary, the saints.
Live with them,
and let your blood flow
for the good of humanity —
like him!
The mass!
It is too great to understand!
His mass, our mass.[11]

On Old Age

One of our spirituality books contains a passage from many years ago, that expresses our view of that kind of natural illness we call old age.

"But in God's sight, where is the greatest beauty: in the child who looks at you with innocent little eyes, so like the clarity of nature and so lively; or in the young girl who glistens with the freshness of a newly-opened flower; or in the wizened and white-haired old man, bent double, almost unable to do anything, perhaps only waiting for death?

"The grain of wheat . . . when, slenderer than a wisp of grass, and bunched together with fellow grains that surround and form the ear, it awaits the time when it

---

11. Chiara Lubich, *Meditations*, pp. 36–37; cf. also *Christian Living Today*, pp. 93–94.

will ripen and be free, alone and independent . . . is beautiful and full of hope!

"It is, however, also beautiful when, ripe at last, it is chosen from among the others because it is better than they, and then, having been buried, it gives life to other ears of wheat. . . .

"But when, shrivelling underground, it reduces its being almost to nothing, grows concentrated, and slowly dies, decaying, to give life to a tiny plant that is distinct from it and yet contains the life of the grain, then, perhaps, it is still more beautiful.

"All various beauties.

"Yet one more beautiful than the other.

"And the last is the most beautiful of all.

"Does God see things in this way?

"Those wrinkles that furrow the little old woman's forehead, that stooped and shaky gait, those brief words full of experience and wisdom, that gentle look of a child and a woman together, but better than both, *is a beauty we do not know.* . . .

"I think God sees like this and that the approach to heaven is far more attractive than the various stages of the long journey of life, which basically serve only to open that door."[12]

On Death

"We think about death," we say, "not in order to have dark thoughts, but thoughts of gold. . . .

---

12. Chiara Lubich, *Meditations,* pp. 113–114; cf. also *Christian Living Today,* pp. 156–158.

"The more we appreciate and go into the depths of suffering, the more we also understand that death is the ultimate offering of ourselves as 'royal priests' here on earth and, therefore, the culmination of our lives."[13]

There can also be joy in thinking of death. At times in our Movement we see it as Saint Francis did, as sister death.

We find this writing: "If the mercy of God grants this, death will mean seeing Mary, seeing Jesus. How then can we surround that passage with mourning, even . . . if it comes with the harsh reality of an agony, be it long or short, and in any case with the breakdown of the human shells of our lives? . . ."[14]

It seems to us that those who see death are those who are watching at the bedside of the one who is dying. Instead, the one who is dying has the adventure of seeing life, because death is the encounter with Christ.

It is a truth of our faith that we will see Jesus immediately after we die, a truth that gives immense consolation. Paul speaks of his "longing to depart this life and be with Christ" (Phil 1:23). Therefore, he speaks of a life with Christ which comes right after death without awaiting the final resurrection (cf. 2 Cor 5:8). So in a way it is true that death does not exist; rather, it is the encounter with the Lord.

But we must prepare ourselves for death before the moment comes.

We should do what Jesus did, who lived for his "hour."

Each one of us also has his own hour.

---

13. Chiara Lubich, *Yes Yes, No No* (London: New City, 1977), p. 91.
14. Unpublished Diary of 14 June 1968.

We should have it foremost in our thoughts as it is foremost in importance in our lives here on earth.

And we should pray for that moment, in the Hail Mary, for example, where we always say, "Pray for us sinners now and at the hour of our death."

So while we are still healthy, we ought to live in expectation of that moment, choosing even now a frame of mind in tune with it: "You, Lord, are my only good" (cf. Ps 16[15]:12).

And we should offer that hour for those things that Jesus has entrusted to us.

If we do so, nothing will take us by surprise.

On the Resurrection

But, in the end, we will rise. We will rise because Jesus is risen. We will rise through the power of the Eucharist, with which we have been nourished during our lives: "Those who eat my flesh and drink my blood have eternal life, and I will raise them up on the last day" (Jn 6:54).

Jesus himself is the resurrection: "I am the resurrection and the life. Those who believe in me, even though they die, will live" (Jn 11:25).

We are linked to him who has been placed as our first brother at the head of us all as we go towards the Father (cf. Rm 8:29).

And how will we rise?

We will rise with our own body and not with another, because each one of us is a unique person, as John Paul II says.[15] We will rise with our bodies, but they will be

---

15. Cf. John Paul II, *Uomo e donna lo creò. Catechesi sull'amore umano* (Rome, 1985), p. 79.

completely different from the way they are now. They will be spiritualized, like the body of the risen Jesus. And we will be, God willing, happy in paradise.

When a relative or a friend of ours leaves for the next life, often people say they are "no longer with us," for they think of them as being lost.

But it should not be like this for us. "Life is changed, not taken away."[16]

The love that our brother or sister had for us — true love because it is rooted in God — remains. Everything passes. Even faith and hope come to an end with the passing of the scene of this world, but love remains (cf. 1 Cor 13:8). God is not so ungenerous with us as to take from us what he himself gave us in our brother or sister.

Those brothers or sisters continue to love us with a love that is now unfaltering.

No, our brothers and sisters are not lost. They are there, as if they had left home to go to another place.

They live in the heavenly homeland and, through God in whom they abide, we can continue to love one another, as the gospel teaches.[17]

The Resurrection and the Cosmos

Speaking of the resurrection, we sometimes express in the Focolare a singular idea with regard to humanity's habitat, that is, the cosmos.

Jesus in his death and resurrection is certainly the true cause of the transformation of the cosmos. But since Paul revealed to us that we men and women

---

16. Preface of the Mass for the dead.
17. Cf. Chiara Lubich, Unpublished Diary of 13 December 1968.

complete the passion of Christ and that nature awaits the revelation of the children of God, it could be true that Jesus also expects the cooperation of people, "Christified" by his eucharist, in order to accomplish the renewal of the cosmos.

If the eucharist is the cause of the resurrection of a human being, is it not possible that the body of a human being, divinized by the eucharist, may be destined to decay underground in order to contribute to the resurrection of the cosmos? We could say, furthermore, that by means of the Eucharistic bread, human beings become "eucharist" for the universe, in the sense that, joined with Christ, they are seeds of the transfiguration of the universe.

We could say, therefore, that the earth eats us up, as we eat the eucharist, not in order to transform us into earth but in order to be itself transformed into the "new heavens and new earth" (Rv 21:1).

In the Focolare we feel strongly that we should take great care of the places where our dead, destined to rise, are laid to rest. The Words of Life[18] that illumined their earthly existence are engraved on their tombs, to the edification of our members who visit the cemetery and read them.

In addition, we would like our cemeteries to be like beautiful gardens in which the tombs convey a message. People pass from one tomb to another and perceive a love that continues. Such an experience has moved some people to tears.

---

18. The reference is to Gospel passages that these people had taken as their personal program for living.

And what will heaven be like? It will be like the earth, but transformed. We do not know if there will be some kind of catastrophe and then the rising of a new earth and new heavens, or if there will be a transformation of the existing universe. We are inclined to think of a transformation of this same earth, of these same heavens.

The universe will continue, it will undergo a transformation, but it will continue and will exist for all eternity. Therefore, it should be viewed in this way even now. When we admire galaxies, sunsets, flowers, pine trees, meadows, and the heavens, we should think, "This will all remain." Human work will also remain, especially if it is the fruit of love, because if it is, it is already purified. These works are made by Jesus within us or among us, and his works last.

These thoughts also enhance the value of ecology, to which people in the Focolare are particularly sensitive. We need to conserve the earth, out of respect, given that it too has a role to play in the future.

One Family

We feel that all the people in our Movement — graced by the Holy Spirit with one of his charisms, which is like a new blood that joins us to one another — are and will remain forever one single family. In this family, some members have already left, so it is a family waiting to be reunited.

In fact, we share the thoughts of Father Alberione, founder of the Saint Pauline congregations:

"*Congregavit nos in unum Christi amor* (the love of Christ has drawn us into one). The same love has gathered our hearts around the heart of Jesus Christ. And so it is with every religious institute; it is not dissolved by death. Consequently, the Congregation can contain members in the Church triumphant, others in the Church purgant, and others in the Church militant here on earth, all of them united by the one bond of love. . . .

"The Congregation is consolidated and perfected through death. As members of a single family in different conditions, we remain united in one goal: glory to God, peace on earth."[19]

On 25 December 1973 I wrote the following words to the Focolarini, and they are still pertinent:

"If I should have to leave this world today, and you were to ask me for a single word, one last word that sums up our Ideal, I would say — certain of being perfectly understood — 'Be a family.'

"Are there among you some who are suffering spiritual or moral trials? Understand them as a mother, and more than a mother would, enlighten them with your words or with your example. Do not leave them feeling the absence of the family warmth, on the contrary, let them feel it all the more.

"Are there some among you who are suffering physically? Let them be your favorites. Suffer with them. Seek to understand their sufferings in depth. Share the fruits of your apostolic endeavors with them so that they may realize that they, more than others, contributed to these fruits.

"Are there some who are dying? Imagine yourself in their place and do for them whatever you would want others to do for you, right to the very end.

---

19. James Alberione, *Mese di esercizi spirituali*, IX, lesson IX.

"Is someone happy because of a particular achievement or for any other reason? Rejoice with him or her so that the consolation may not be spoiled and that person's heart not be closed, but that the joy may spread to all.

"Is someone leaving? Don't let him or her go without a heart filled with this single legacy: a sense of the family, so that they may take it with them wherever they go.

"Never put any kind of activity — neither spiritual nor apostolic — before generating a family spirit with those brothers or sisters you live with.

"And wherever you go to bring the ideal of Christ, to extend the immense family of the Work of Mary, you can do nothing better than to seek to create with discretion, with prudence, but with determination, the family spirit. It is a spirit that is humble, that desires the good of the others, that is not proud . . . it is . . . charity which is true and complete.

"In short, if I should have to leave you, I would have Jesus in me repeat to you: 'Love one another . . . so that all may be one.' "[20]

And now, in line with the new will of God expressed to us by the Church in the person of John Paul II on the vigil of Pentecost 1998 in Saint Peter's Square,[21] I would say: widen this family spirit to include all the existing Movements and Ecclesial Communities. Offer your love to all the religious families who with us repre-

20. Chiara Lubich, Writing of 25 December 1973; in *La dottrina spirituale*, pp. 86–87.
21. On that day the new Ecclesial Movements and Communities, most of which had come into existence after Vatican II, gathered together for the first time. The Pope invited them to a new ecclesial maturity, and Chiara Lubich expressed her own commitment to work in a special way for communion among all these groups.

sent the charismatic aspect of the Church. At the same time, do not hesitate to extend it generously to Christ who lives in all those who represent the institutional aspect of the Church, so that the "Church-communion" may be a reality in the third millennium. And let us not forget those who are outside of the Church, in the world, that world for whom Jesus came and we are called to inflame.

Conclusion

The Focolare's charism of unity has always made us tend, with regard to all the aspects of our life, to think big, so to speak. In this context, for example, the charism led us to consider not only physical but also spiritual health, and not only personal but also collective health.

In fact, to this aspect of health we link such spiritual realities as the presence of Jesus in our midst and the most holy eucharist.

Jesus in our midst is linked to this aspect because the perfect health of our soul lies in his presence among us. Our characteristic spirituality demands that we do not seek to attain spiritual health on our own. As human beings and as Christians, we are ourselves only in relationship with others. It is in relating to others, in loving our neighbors, that each of us becomes fully the person we are, that is, Jesus, another Jesus. For this reason, in order to claim to be spiritually healthy, that is, complete, perfect, fulfilled, in the fullness of joy, we must love others to the point of generating the presence of Jesus in our midst.

The eucharist is linked to this aspect, furthermore, not only because it is the cause of our resurrection, in which our physical and spiritual health will become perfect and lasting, but also because it is through the eucharist that we become one body and one blood with Christ. The eucharist transforms us all into the Christ we receive; it makes us Christ and for this reason it is our spiritual health.

Love Creates a Home

Father Tommasi,[1] who was asked by the Archbishop of Trent, Carlo de Ferrari, to supervise the early development of the Focolare, once said, when it became apparent that there was a gift of the Spirit in the light that guided us, that it was "a charism that God has poured down upon earth, a gift that gives shape to a society on the model of the Holy Trinity."

He had hit the mark. That is how it is. Our ideal is the Mystical Body of Christ lived out, made tangible. The seven aspects are different ways of looking at this fact, at least insofar as it is realized in our Movement.

If the first aspect considers the Mystical Body as communion of all the members that compose it, the second contemplates it in the radiance it sheds abroad. If the third aspect highlights how the members individually and as a group are rooted in God, the fourth considers the One who links one member to another: Christ among them.

The fifth aspect — the one we will consider now — enters more deeply into the reality of the Mystical Body, into the relationship of each member with the other, and of all with their head, Christ. It is this aspect that, to simplify things and identify them with the colors of the rainbow, we call the "blue" or *ecclesia*.

---

1. Giovanni Tommasi, superior general of the Stigmatine Fathers.

In this aspect we see the Mystical Body as Church; we think of the church buildings that accommodate it, the houses that shelter it, and the clothes that dress its members.

The Beauty of Mary

I wrote in 1955, twelve years after the birth of the Focolare Movement: "If we put all these aspects together, what do they show? The beauty of Mary, of the Work of Mary. They are the new wineskins that contain a new spirit, which is the charism that God gave us. They are like new songs that resound in all the communities of the Movement whether they be large or small."[2]

When these aspects emerged, they appeared as the first supports of the heavenly structure of our Movement, and they were immediately included in the brief Statutes, which at that time we called our Rule. Ever since then the Holy Spirit has emphasized the importance, the value, of the Statutes or Rule.

In that same text, we read: "Some people say that the Rule poses limits. . . . But this is not so. The Rule channels the spirit so that it does not waver and fade. We can liken the spirit to a little flame. If it is not sheltered in a hearth, it dies out at the first gust of wind.

"The Rule for us means giving a summary of everything, being 'consumed in one,' and being accountable to the person who represents Jesus for us (here on earth) for what has been entrusted to us, because it is and should be part of the whole."

---

2. Chiara Lubich, Unpublished Talk, "How the Seven Aspects Came About," Milan, 13 April 1955.

Looking to the Origins: Seeds for a New Culture

But let's return to our topic.

During the early days, the Holy Spirit helped us to see at once the magnitude of the Movement that was coming to life, for instance, when he made clear its specific aim: to contribute to realizing the prayer of Jesus, "May they all be one" (naturally, doing this together with the Church). But he also began to suggest very simple ideas concerning persons with particular vocations (like the men and women Focolarini). These ideas were immediately taken into consideration in order to realize the goals of the Holy Spirit, not so much by offering theories, but by making people live in a specific way right from the start.

Among the first ideas are those concerning their home, the focolare house, and their clothing.

However, because the men and women Focolarini are called, through the charism of unity, to become another Christ, and their coming together is a living out of the Mystical Body of Christ, the essential ideas and guiding principles as to where they live and the way they dress can be a light for everyone in the various branches of the Focolare Movement. Fundamentally, they have an identical calling, and this is written in their specific guidelines.

The charism of unity is a new charism, and it gives rise not only to a new spiritual life, which everyone can live, but also to a new culture, which can be present in everyone.

Our Houses

With regard to where the Focolarini live, the focolares, we had precise and detailed ways of going about things from the early years of our Movement. In the Rule written in 1951, we read: "Every focolare should be a replica of the little house of Nazareth. It should look like a home where a family lives."

It is the first actualization of that well-known intuition I had at Loreto in 1939:[3] that what was coming to life would have something to do with the little house of Nazareth, with Jesus in the midst of Mary and Joseph.

Later on we commented: "If ours is the dwelling place of true members of a family united in the name of Jesus, if it is an environment that contains a family whose brother is Christ himself . . . the house that shelters us will be truly 'home.' "

IN THE SCRIPTURES

The home has always been important in Christian spiritualities.

Carlo Carretto,[4] a Little Brother of Jesus who was very well known at least in Italy, wrote about his attraction for a home even though his spiritual formation took place in the desert:

---

3. When she was taking a course for Catholic Action leaders, Chiara Lubich felt strongly drawn to the "house of Nazareth," the little house in Loreto in which, tradition holds, the holy family lived. There she became convinced that her path in life was connected to what had existed in that house, and that many would follow her.
4. Carlo Carretto, president of the GIAC (Italian Youth of Catholic Action) from 1946 to1953, lived for a long time in the Sahara Desert as a Little Brother of Jesus. Later he founded the Little Brothers of the Gospel at Spello, Italy, and wrote a number of influential books on spirituality.

"God is my Father. . . . With him I have the gift of life. . . . Above all, with him I have the gift of a 'home.' To have a home, to live in a home. . . . We are made for a home where there is a father and where there are brothers and sisters. . . . We are made for a home that gives us a sense of stability, continuity, and rest."[5]

Moreover, in scripture the Church itself is referred to as a home or house. Paul says: "I hope to come to you soon, but I am writing these instructions to you so that, if I am delayed, you may know how one ought to behave in the household of God, which is the church of the living God, the pillar and bulwark of the truth" (1 Tim 3:14–15).

Again, speaking of Christ, he says: "We are his house if we hold firm the confidence and the pride that belong to hope" (Heb 3:6).

Jesus even compares heaven to a house: "In my Father's house there are many dwelling places. If it were not so, would I have told you that I go to prepare a place for you?" (Jn 14:2).

And Carlo Carretto continues: "John speaks of a house in the Book of Revelation, when he sees the end of time in a vision that sums up the messianic realities: 'And I saw the holy city, the new Jerusalem, coming down out of heaven from God, prepared as a bride adorned for her husband. And I heard a loud voice from the throne saying, "See, the home of God is among mortals. He will dwell with them as their God; they will be his peoples, and God himself will be with them" ' (Rev 21:2–3).

---

5. Carlo Carretto, *Ogni giorno un pensiero* (Rome: Città Nuova, 1993), p. 211.

"Yes, God will dwell with the human race in the same 'home' and his presence will be so total that it will exclude any previous 'presence,' even that of the Temple: 'I saw no temple in the city, for its temple is the Lord God the Almighty and the Lamb' (Rev 21:22)."[6]

LIKE THE HOUSE OF NAZARETH

We wrote in 1951: "There should be nothing in our homes that resembles an office or a hotel. Everything should be luminous, warm, and orderly, like the order of all that comes from the hand of God.

"The focolare should be beautiful like nature: like a meadow, like the sky."[7]

In 1960 we find written: "We have a home, too, a place to live, like Our Lady had in the little house of Nazareth — she had a home. I wouldn't know how to tell you with what taste things should be arranged . . . but undoubtedly a new harmony is asked of us.

"We may only have a few things, but they will be placed in such a way that they will please everyone . . . and whoever comes will feel forced to say: 'There is nothing special in this house, and yet I feel at home. . . .'

"[It will be the same] harmony that the Creator imprinted in nature. It is the harmony of our souls united in God . . . imprinted in our surroundings, in our focolares . . . in our meeting rooms, in our headquarters and, one day, in our churches."[8]

---

6. Carretto, *Ogni giorno un pensiero*, p. 394.
7. Chiara Lubich, *Parole di sapienza* (unpublished).
8. Chiara Lubich, Unpublished Talk, *"Aspetti della vita di focolare,"* 12 June 1960.

The reason for keeping our house in a certain way became clear to us in 1964 when we read something written by Thomas à Kempis. Meditating on the birth of Jesus in the grotto of Bethlehem, he said the following:

"Oh! how venerable is this place! . . . Enter, my soul, into this poor dwelling of the heavenly king. . . . Observe how the newly born God-Man lies silently in the manger. . . .

"Adore God here. . . . Meditate on the tender, loving gestures of the Virgin Mary, how great her joy must be, how sublime her contemplation of the son to whom she has given birth. . . .

"Consider everything as if you were in their presence (and say):

" 'I will stay here to serve my Lord, the Lady Mary and St Joseph her guardian. I will light the fire and look after it with care; I will prepare the meal and fetch the water. I will clean out the courtyard, sweep the house, mend the cracks to protect it from the wind and rain. . . . Then I will gather roses and lilies. . . . I will decorate the holy cradle. . . . I will open the window of the manger so that daylight will shine everywhere and the holy angels will descend from above and fill this house with gentle rejoicing.' "[9]

This passage from Thomas à Kempis helped us then, as it does today, to understand how an inner attitude of reverence and affection cannot help but be reflected on external surroundings as well.

---

9. Thomas à Kempis, *Sermones de vita et passione Dominis*, in vol. 3 of *Opera Omnia*, M. Pohl, ed. (Freiburg i. Br., 1904), pp. 91–104 (passim).

And we know that our attitude must be love, love for God and, out of love for him, love for our brothers and sisters.

And therefore in this, as in every aspect of our life, we must be guided by love, and when our love is directed to our brothers and sisters, it leads us to making ourselves one with them.

Consequently, our house will not necessarily be poor or poorer than others. We can live in a palace or in a "*mocambo*," in a skyscraper or in a country cottage. We can live anywhere, so long as our surroundings are an expression of love for our brothers and sisters.

Our Statutes state that "our house should suit the surroundings where most of our apostolic endeavors are carried out," and this too is done out of love.

MARY'S TASTE

Among those early thoughts about our houses, one was frequently mentioned: we need to look after them with "Mary's taste."

Certainly, it is rather difficult to know what Mary's taste was like. We believe, however, that we will be able to understand and apply it only if unity is lived among the members of the focolare and with the rest of the Movement. In this way, we can hope to be, at least in this particular detail, an expression of the whole Work of Mary, which is called to repeat and continue the presence of Mary in the world today.

Perhaps we can understand the idea of beauty that often appears in the notes written about our houses if we remember that Mary is the "All Beautiful One."

Our houses will have to be modern because they should always be in tune with the times.

Moreover, it is important that our houses be built to last (indeed, they are often the property of the Work of Mary). The Benedictine abbeys, scattered here and there in the world, have endured, even though thousands of monks have spent their lives in them, and the same should apply to our houses.

In fact, a reflection of God's plan for a given religious family is imprinted upon their houses. And so future generations who are called to the same family, as they move from one part of the house to another, will be able to understand how to live all the aspects of their life — aspects which were taken into consideration in building the house and in arranging its different areas. Thus, the house itself will help them to live all these aspects and not neglect any of them.

TAKING CARE OF OUR HOUSES AND BEING DETACHED FROM THEM

With regard to this aspect of love, however, we also find the following suggestion. An inventory of our houses should be made. It will be helpful above all for the person in charge of the zone who, knowing how things are for everyone, will be able to arrange a sharing of furniture or other items among the focolares. Not only will this help everyone to be detached from things, but it will also keep alive the creativity that enables them to re-arrange the remaining furniture in a new harmony.

The Focolarini should also know how to look after their house, take care of their clothes, and cook meals so that, if possible, it is never necessary to have people outside of their "family" to do such tasks.

Indeed, the men and women Focolarini, whatever their profession, should be happy to be seen by anyone with an apron on, happy to set the table, to clear away the dishes, and so on. This too is a part of their vocation. We know of young people who felt the call to give their lives to God after seeing the Focolarini carrying out these very tasks.

What matters is not what we do: what matters is that it is Jesus in us who does it, and he is present if we are a living expression of his will.

In spite of all this love for one's house, since our ideal is and always remains God, the Spirit also suggested that we be detached from our house, reminding us of the words of Jesus: "Foxes have holes, and birds of the air have nests; but the Son of Man has nowhere to lay his head" (Mt 8:20).

For the Focolarini, who are called to go to every part of the world to bring our ideal, this detachment is essential, having to adapt themselves, at least for a certain period of time, to everything.

Detachment is also necessary for those whose vocation involves making the Christian community visible, like our Volunteers,[10] for example. God wants them to be committed to "making available to the Work of Mary the places where they live and the houses they own for meetings, gatherings and conferences, so as to allow the Focolare's spirit to enter more effectively into the midst of the world."

------

10. A branch of the Focolare Movement made up of two parts: the men and women Volunteers. They are "persons committed to bring back the presence of God, the source of freedom and unity, to the widest range of environments in society."

In a sense, the focolare must also be a church, a temple, the temple of the living God, not because of external images (even though they may be present in any family), but for the constant, silent, constructive, fruitful presence of God among persons united in the name of Jesus.

An article written in the 1950s, which I have adapted for this occasion, says:

I believe there is no man's heart, still less a woman's, that has not at least once, especially in youth, felt the attraction of the cloister.

It is not the attraction of a cloistered way of life, but of something that seems to be concentrated there, between those four walls, something that makes itself felt, resounding deeply, even from a distance.

In these communities, with which the world, thank God, is strewn like a dark night dotted with constellations, there is the light of the presence of God. . . .

Though sunken in silence, these houses . . . through the mysterious power of celestial things, speak to the hearts of human beings and utter a voice unknown to the world: a blessedness of union with God that humanity longs for.

Yet also the focolare, small abode in the midst of others, can have the perfume of the cloister; also the walls where I live can become a kingdom of peace, God's fortress in the midst of the world.

The external noise of the television of the tenant next door, or the roar of the traffic, or the noise of people on the streets take away none of its enchantment. The mutual love which brings about the presence of Jesus among those brothers or sisters takes possession of their whole existence and gives to their walls the sacredness of an abbey, the solemnity of a church, to their sitting at table the sweetness of a ritual, to their clothes the perfume of a blessed habit, to the sound of the doorbell or the telephone the joyous note of a meeting with other brothers or sisters, which interrupts, yet continues, their unity in God.

Then, upon the silence of their ego, Another will speak and, upon their extinguishing themselves, a light will be lit. And it will shine afar, passing beyond and almost consecrating those walls that protect a living cell of the Body of Christ. And other people will come to the focolare to seek the Lord with them, and in their shared, loving search, the flame will grow, the divine melody will rise a tone. Christ will be their cloister, the Christ of their hearts, Christ in the midst of their hearts.[11]

From the "Lauretanas" to Little Towns

In a diary from 1966 we read that some focolares had opened up like flowers, creating new spaces suitable for specific functions of the Focolare Movement. These were houses not only for the Focolarini but also for those in positions of responsibility within the Movement.

We called them "Lauretanas."[12]

---

11. Cf. Chiara Lubich, *Meditations*, pp. 94–95, cf. also *Christian Living Today*, pp. 149–151.
12. The term "*Lauretana*" refers to Loreto, where there is the house that is traditionally held to have been the home of the Holy Family. Hence a "*Lauretana*" is a "House of Loreto," a building that reflects the home of the Holy Family.

They were larger than the ordinary focolares but with the same basic vocation, that of having Jesus among the members, a contemplative and active vocation at one and the same time. This can be seen from a song of that time, entitled:

A Little Castle of Gold
A miracle of love
Seen only by the angels,
A dream within Mary's heart,
A humble flower among all flowers
Hiding a holy mystery —
O House of Loreto!
Enchanted by our first love,
Our hearts so close to God
Reigning among us all,
In a little castle of gold
Fragrant with flowers rare —
O House of Loreto!
Now in our hearts Mary lives again

Here Virgin, Mother, Spouse,[13]
New fount of Beautiful Love,
Only dawn of all hope;
Life is contemplation here —
O House of Loreto!

In a diary from 1967 we find this concept: "*All* the Focolarini should contribute to keeping the *lauretana* as we imagine Mary kept her home. . . . And surely Jesus

---

13. In the House of Loreto, that is, the "*lauretana* house," "Mary lives again . . . Virgin, Mother, Spouse" through the presence of men and women Focolarini, some of whom are celibate and others married.

and Joseph helped her." Everyone should help, including the Focolarino responsible for the focolare, including the Focolarina responsible for the entire Work of Mary. This is required by our spirit. Why? Because we are all brothers and sisters.

We read, "Love will make . . . Christian brotherhood shine in its characteristic beauty so that whoever visits the focolare house will always be able to say: 'How very good and pleasant it is when brothers live together in unity!' (Ps 133:1)."

As time went on the *lauretanas* grew and became regional centers, with office space for the aspects, the branches, the dialogues, and various activities, and so on.[14]

But it was always Jesus among us who had to be our guide, our source of light to lead us in serving the Work of God.

To sum up we have permanent focolares for the Focolarini, whether they be lay people or priests; and temporary focolares, that is, nucleuses, for Volunteers, priests, and religious, and units for the Gen, Gen seminarians, and Gen religious.[15]

Then, we have the *lauretanas*, the regional centers.

And this is not all, we have Mariapolis Centers and temporary little towns, like the Mariapolises that take

---

14. This is a reference to structures and activities of the Focolare Movement, for example, its work in ecumenical and interreligious dialogue; its publishing houses like New City Press and the twenty-five others throughout the world; its international musical groups, Gen Rosso and Gen Verde.

15. "Gen" stands for New *Gen*eration, the Focolare Movement's youth branch.

place during the summer and, so far twenty permanent little towns throughout the world.[16]

More time would be needed to explain all this: it is a matter of growth, of development of this aspect of love at the service of the Work of Mary.

Our Clothing: "Consider the Lilies of the Field"

The Holy Spirit has also suggested guidelines for our way of dressing, the clothing that we wear. They reflect our gospel-based spirituality, based on the Mystical Body. They are guidelines for the Focolarini, but they are applicable to all who belong to the Work of Mary.

While our houses are an expression of the Movement insofar as it is a collectivity of persons, a new family born in the Church, the clothes we wear indicate the presence of a member of this family who, if he or she is truly a living part of this community, is nothing other than another Christ.

Religious families, the result of new charisms in the Church, have always given attention to this detail, and so we have countless ways of dressing.

----

16. *Mariapolis Centers* are meeting places, in many of the Movement's regions or zones, for people from all parts of the Movement.
Temporary little towns or *Mariapolises* are open meetings run by the Focolare in which people can experience for a few days what it is like if the Gospel is lived together.
Permanent little towns or *Mariapolises* are a small piece of society that, when they are complete, contains every aspect of human life, from houses to work places, from churches to spaces for leisure. They are a picture of how society could be if renewed by the Gospel, and they contain schools for the training of the members of the Movement. The number (twenty) of such little towns mentioned in the text above was correct at the time of writing, but they are increasing. At the time of this book's publication there are now thirty-three.

Our little 1951 Rule gives us this pointer:

"It seems that we can understand what God wants from the Focolarini, in this field too, if we look at their nature. Their vocation is to be 'children,' 'sons' and 'daughters.' They are persons born knowing that they have a Father, believing in love, living in the arms of the love of God, and so their outward appearance is that which is given them by a Father who is God, a God who is the creator of the universe. Their style will be his, and we know that the imprint of God on creation is all harmony.

"The clothes of the Focolarini should be like the clothing God has given to nature. And the passage of the Gospel that should inspire them is: 'Consider the lilies of the field, how they grow . . . yet I tell you, even Solomon in all his glory was not clothed like one of these' (Mt 6:28–29).

"Therefore, the clothing of the Focolarini should show that they are children of God, children of the Creator of nature, children of the Lord of creation."[17]

To be dressed like the lilies of the field means to be dressed in a way that has freshness and taste, just as the flowers are fresh and beautiful. But also, since our clothes cover a person who is a temple of the Holy Spirit, they must have the imprint of the divine, so they will be characterized by dignified good taste and moderation, by elegance and simplicity, because we are children of God; and by modesty because we are children of Mary; without extravagance, without expensive jewellery, because real value lies in the beauty of the person, inflamed with the love of God.

---

17. Cf. Chiara Lubich, Unpublished Diary, 25 August 1980 (quoting the 1951 Rule).

In this regard, it is interesting to note how the virgins in the early days of Christianity dressed. None wore gold, silver, precious stones or pearls, because they had a genuine disregard for riches.

This made us wonder about our focolares, the *lauretanas*, and so on: are they luxuriant? Could they appear to be luxuriant because they contain valuable furniture or other articles? If the answer is yes, we must sell these things and give the money to the poor. The focolares should be hospitable, certainly, but there should be nothing elaborate.

The first virgins were dressed like others because they had to live in the midst of the world. If they were rich, they gave away everything they had. We should take on this same attitude, especially now in times of consumerism.

And these thoughts still need to be stressed.

The Focolarini are not to have a uniform. They are to dress as ordinary people, without religious signs, so that they cannot be singled out from others, but are like them, hidden in the midst of the crowd.

BEING GUIDED BY LOVE

Love should also be our guide in the way we dress.

The Focolarini are born to love. They remain in the world without being of the world, to love their fellow human beings, and their way of dressing must aid them in this task. To enter into conversation with the world it is necessary to look like everyone else — guidance that is not be taken lightly. In a community of consecrated persons, where humanly speaking no one has to please anyone else, it would be easy to neglect one's personal appearance. And, if many or all do the same, we would soon have a uniform: "Look, there go the . . . You can tell who they are by the way they dress, by how shabby they are . . ." And at this point, where have dignified good taste and a becoming appearance gone? Where is the simplicity that is true elegance?

Showing the Beauty of God

The Holy Spirit made yet another suggestion to us. Since the world around us is far from God and has often reached the point of being against the Church (partly because it sees only the deformed view given by our lives that are not really Christian), it would be helpful to display not only the Church's goodness and truth, but also, by means of the places where we live and the way in which we dress, its beauty.

Thinking of all these guidelines we have often wanted to give a definition of the way the Focolarini dress that could apply in our times and in future centuries. It is a definition that we feel is universal and so suited to the majority of the Focolare Movement's members. It is this: we ought to dress as Jesus and Mary would dress in every period of history, in every particular setting.

Since this is the first time that the vocation of the Focolarini is appearing on earth, and since, in association with other brothers and sisters, it is the first time that a society of this kind is being offered to the world, probably the guidelines for its houses and way of dressing should be new too.

And just as our spirituality, with its emerging doctrine, is spreading far and wide, so too the Focolarini's way of dressing will eventually have to spread and offer a new line of fashion. And this is already happening.

In a similar way, from the style of the houses of the Focolarini there could emerge ideas for a renewed architecture; and here too something is beginning to happen.

Love Generates Wisdom

Just as love lived by the members of the Movement creates communion, radiates, uplifts, heals, creates a home, it also generates light and wisdom.

In the history of the Focolare there is a very well-known event that we have always held to be a fundamental and founding moment for this aspect.

I refer to that day in the 1940s, in the first focolare of Piazza Cappuccini, Trent, when I left the books I loved so much, putting them in the attic.

By doing this I was resolving a contradiction I felt had become clear in my life: seeking the truth in philosophy while truth is wholly present in the eucharistic Jesus I received every morning.

In fact, a light of the Holy Spirit had made me understand clearly that I would find the truth, the full, authentic, indisputable, sublime, and profound truth, in him, *the* Truth: "I am the way and the truth and the life" (Jn 14:6).

"I Saw a Light"

This episode, I believe, marks the beginning of the aspect we are dealing with here.

I recently found in our archives a letter I wrote to a friend during those early days.

"Look, I am a person passing through this world.

"I have seen many beautiful and good things and I have always been attracted only by them.

"One day (one indefinable day), I saw a light. It seemed to me to be more beautiful than the other beautiful things, and I followed it.

"I realized that it was the Truth."

This letter surprised me: why, I wondered, was I able to say such a thing? And I came to the conclusion that the light I spoke about was the charism given to us by the Holy Spirit and which later the Church studied and, using its gift of discernment, approved.

What I have found interesting in the writings, talks, and diary entries about this sixth aspect which, to keep things simple, I will call the indigo, is that they are not usually lengthy thoughts that have been fully worked out and elaborated. They are drops, perhaps of wisdom or of sound human judgement, that add to or explain more completely things that are already known. Or they are just the drawing out of the consequences of what we think, but I have chosen them and wished to highlight them simply because, being beautiful, they have in themselves, I think, a ray of that beauty which is, at the same time, the truth of God. Others are predictions that are astounding because, years and years later, they have been fulfilled.

Assisi, Paris, Hollywood

We can look at the 1950s. In 1954 the Holy Spirit illuminated us about the seven aspects of love, and since 1955 we have spoken about the indigo. And then something happened which surprised us very much: it seemed as if, from that point on, the Holy Spirit wished to communicate to us his plans for our Movement. He made us understand that, in the course of time, there would be three moments in the Work of Mary, defined by these names: Assisi, Paris and Hollywood. They were already in Focolare DNA, so to speak, because of the charism that had brought it about and had always guided it, but they came to light fully only a few decades later.

It was something I would bring up again only in 1988.[1] I said:

"In our Movement, we can single out three periods: the first occurred when our spirituality, our lifestyle, was born. And we called it 'Assisi.'

"The second period came when I began to study in order to compare the aspects of our spirituality with the doctrine of the Church. We saw that they matched up with each other, while foreseeing that this would also open up new horizons. I shared this with everyone.

"In this regard, we were deeply affected and also somewhat fearful because of a remark attributed to Saint Francis, who was concerned that his friars might become attached to books: 'Paris, Paris, you destroy Assisi.' "

We affirmed: "We want Paris, but also Assisi. We live our spirituality, but we want to study too."

And now, the third period has already opened up, one that we have given the title of another symbolic place: Hollywood. It presents and will present to the public the message of our Movement through various art forms and through the media.

Let's address our theme more directly now.

---

1. These are excerpts from spoken talks adapted for written presentation.

What is Wisdom?

We quote the following section from a book of 1964 that we liked very much. It was written by the theologian Father Raimondo Spiazzi:

"The gift of wisdom puts the soul in contact with eternal realities. . . . It scrutinizes the depths of God and discerns his radiant beauty. The soul beholds that which it cannot repeat, and without ever being quenched it drinks from this exhaustible source with an ever-growing desire, as a deer longs for streams of water.

"But, having discovered and almost tasted God, with this light in its eyes, the soul is able to look at the world and to see it clearly . . . judging everything from a divine viewpoint, almost projecting over everything the light of God's infinite gaze.

"In the mind of a wise Christian there is, as it were, a reconstruction of the ideal order that exists in the mind of God. The unfolding of eras and ages, the interwoven course of events, the flow of things, the historical process, the development of its own life all are seen from the perspective of their dependence-convergence relationship to a divine plan . . . having the same mental synthesis as God who sees each thing in the Word, who loves each thing in the Spirit, and who knows all by loving, and loves all in the very act of his infinite contemplation."[2]

"A member of the Movement must possess wisdom." We stated this and repeated it in our writings, in our various Statutes. We considered it a command.

------

2. R. Spiazzi, *Lo Spirito Santo e la vita cristiana* (Rome, 1964), p. 229.

But we might wonder: how is it possible to "command" wisdom?

The same Holy Spirit who commands something (through the Statutes he inspired), also gives us the answer.

And in time, the answer became increasingly clear for us.

HOW TO ACQUIRE WISDOM

We can acquire wisdom in four ways: by asking God for it, by loving God and neighbor, by loving Jesus forsaken, and by bringing Jesus into our midst.

1) We have always prayed for wisdom, ever since the earliest days, I would say, when to prepare ourselves to speak before the small audiences of that time we sometimes stayed even an hour in front of Jesus in the tabernacle. We would repeat to him, "You are everything, I am nothing," so that he, and he alone, would speak through us. This is how everything began, and we should remember this.

Still today we pray to the Father, fairly frequently using a prayer we call a *consenserint*. As is widely known, this is the name we give to the prayer taught us by Jesus when he said: "If two of you agree on earth about anything you ask, it will be done for you by my Father in heaven" (Mt 18:19). We often pray together like this before giving a talk, in order to have the Holy Spirit.

2) Another way to acquire wisdom is by loving: by loving God and neighbor.

It has always been our conviction, proven by experience, that loving brings light. In fact, right from the beginning, these words of Jesus have had a special place

150

in our hearts: "They who have my commandments and keep them are those who love me; and those who love me will be loved by my Father, and I will love them and *reveal myself* to them" (Jn 14:21).

Saint Bede said: "To the one who has love for the Word [in which Christ is present], will also be given the intelligence to understand the Word that he loves; while the one who does not love the Word will have no taste whatsoever for the delights of true wisdom. Even if he believes he possesses it, as a result of natural gifts and study, he will not possess it."[3]

"To have wisdom," we used to explain, "it is necessary to be another Jesus, and to be another Jesus it is necessary to love: the light that comes from loving is wisdom." As a bicycle light comes on when you pedal, so wisdom lights up in us when we love.

We would recall an Oriental proverb: "Give me your heart [that is, love] and I will give you a pair of eyes," which means: love, and I will make you see.

We have wisdom, therefore, by loving.

3) We also acquire wisdom by loving Jesus crucified and forsaken.

In Chapter Four of our current Statutes, it says: "The persons who are part of the Work of Mary will try to have true Christian wisdom before anything else: 'For God loves nothing so much as the person who lives with wisdom' (Wis 7:28).

"For this reason, embracing Christ's cross and forsakenness with him, they will try to make the Risen Lord shine out in their hearts. It is he who pours out the gifts of the Spirit" (art. 58).

---

3. Bede, *Commento al Vangelo di Marco*, vol. 1 (Rome, 1970), p. 129.

I had already said in 1967 that we have wisdom when we love Jesus forsaken:

"If we do not love the cross, if we do not live only by means of it, then in our hearts there is no true love for God and for our brothers and sisters, nor is there wisdom.

"As we did when we had scarcely been born to this new life, we repeat the same words each morning when offering up our day: 'Because you are forsaken Jesus, because you are desolate Mary.' And Jesus forsaken is the totality of wisdom for us."[4]

We read in the letters of Bernard of Clairvaux what he once said to a professor in Paris: "I have heard that you comment on the books of the Prophets. But can you truly say that you understand their lessons and, more importantly, their teaching on Christ? You would understand Christ better by following him than by teaching about him."

Louis de Montfort almost identifies wisdom with the cross. From him we understand that the tree of the cross distills from itself eternal nectar; that is, wisdom, a ray, a reflection, a participation in the eternal Wisdom which is the Word of God.

He says that suffering teaches things that cannot be learned from any other art. It holds the highest teaching chair. Suffering is a teacher of wisdom, and the one who has wisdom is blessed. Blessed, in fact, are the ones who are suffering. They will be consoled not only with their reward in the next life but with the contemplation of heavenly things in this life.[5]

---

4. Chiara Lubich, Unpublished Diary, 17 May 1967.
5. L. G. Montfort, *Amore dell' Eterna Sapienza*, n. 180.

4) The fourth way to have wisdom is by having Jesus in our midst.

"Moreover," continue the Statutes, "they will strive to be united so that Christ who is present where there is mutual love may pour forth among them the gifts of the Spirit" (art. 58).

We are more and more convinced that "we must have wisdom individually (through the risen Lord in us) and collectively (with Jesus among us). From this we have to learn to be 'fountains that overflow.' "

A typical sign of someone speaking with wisdom is a listener's exclamation, "How beautiful!" Such a comment is never in reference to a purely human way of reasoning, but to something that is supernatural. For example, if our words are able to show the golden thread that links the events of our lives, filling us with admiration, it means that there is wisdom present.

And there has been abundant wisdom in our Movement, in outlining both its spirituality and its structure.

THE ONE TEACHER

As we often recall, even before our adventure of living the spirituality of unity, I had wanted to know God, and I seemed to have heard these words in my heart: "I will be your Teacher."

And he really has been a teacher for me and for many others.

This is why I was able to say at the University of Buenos Aires in 1998:

"It is with surprise that I can affirm now, only for the glory of God, that after decades spent in following this splendid and demanding way, the Lord, in his goodness, led me and those who are part of the Focolare to know something of his infinite wisdom. This did not involve only the study of God, theology, but also, so it would seem, other realms of knowledge, thus giving us an insight into how we can renew the different disciplines of human knowledge from within, in order to make them authentic, true and pleasing to him."[6]

In this regard, we would like to recall what is written in the Book of Wisdom:

> Although she is but one, she can do all things,
> and while remaining in herself,
> she renews all things. . . .
> She is more beautiful than the sun,
> and excels every constellation of the stars.
> Compared with the light she is found to be superior,
> for it is succeeded by the night,
> but against wisdom
> evil does not prevail.
> (Wis 7:27–30)

Study

STUDY AT THE SERVICE OF WISDOM

Let us now speak about study.

Study is necessary but under one condition: "The indigo is not so much study as wisdom because it is a color of love, love that becomes wisdom, that illuminates."

Study is not something added on to wisdom but a means of amplifying it, of making it more radiant. "The

---

6. Chiara Lubich, lecture given on the occasion of the reception of the doctorate *honoris causa* in humanities, Buenos Aires, 6 April 1998.

alpha and omega," we continue to read, "is always wisdom. The origin is wisdom and the end is wisdom: God."

We also made clear the place of study: "Study is . . . the footstool of wisdom."

In any case, study is important for us. We always knew that "to increase wisdom it is necessary to study."

And, thanks be to God, so far it appears that "Paris has not destroyed Assisi." Study has been at the service of wisdom.

The following writing, too, encourages study: "But it could be much more (at the service of wisdom). A seventh part of our life (thinking of the seven aspects of love) should always be devoted to study."

As early as 1960 we find written:

"Wisdom will be supported and equipped by the knowledge of theology and of any other secular knowledge that may be useful.

"Theology, however, should never suffocate wisdom but, rather, theology should help wisdom."

And we insisted:

"I was filled with joy at the thought that in our Movement study is viewed as one of the seven expressions of our life, as an aspect of love. This can be so, however, on the condition that it serves our love of God and neighbor. Otherwise study is an obstacle; it is Paris destroying Assisi."

"INUNDATIONS"

There is a comment (among the many) that makes it clear how study even in the fields of the sciences and the humanities is also something that God specifically wants of us. In time, this point proved to be true, and especially now in view of the so-called "inundations."[7]

With regard to the studies of the Focolarini, for example, we said as early as 1966:

"As far studies in the fields of science and the humanities are concerned, the Focolarini should keep up to date on their professional knowledge and should always improve it.

"We should keep in mind that as time passes many Focolarini with the same profession will come together to work in the projects that will be set up. Consequently, they will have to put in common, with Jesus in their midst, the ideas and insights they will have acquired day by day.

"The presence of Jesus in the midst of those who work in the same field will enhance the presence of Jesus in that sector, and it will also enlighten that field of work itself.

"At the same time, these Focolarini will be able to be leaven in Centers of the Movement [that deal with specific 'inundations']."

OUR THEOLOGY

"With regard to theological studies, we foresee the Focolarini attending courses at the level of higher education."

And there is a thought that frequently recurs:

---

7. The term "inundations," from "the streams of living water" in John Chrysostom (*In Johannem homilia*, 51, PG 59, 294), is intended to signify the penetration of the life and light of the charism of unity into various human activities.

"With regard to theology, we ought to focus on the doctrine of the Body of Christ." This should be studied and perfected in every detail.

"The resulting legacy will be shared with others in the Work of Mary and will also be an enrichment for the Church."

And this is linked to another important concept:

"Naturally, the doctrine of the Body of Christ (which implies living in accordance with the Trinitarian model) will have repercussions also on the whole of society which then, at least for those who work in the Work of Mary, will be built in the image and likeness of the Body of Christ."

How to Study

With regard to the way of studying, in 1974 a seminarian asked me the following question: "How can we study theology without the risk of being overwhelmed by it or of losing sight of our total commitment to the ideal and to the gospel?" I replied:

"It's very simple. I, too, studied, and I was told fourteen times to stop and then to start again.

"I remember the last hour I spent studying. I'll never forget it. I was sitting on a rug on the floor, with an atlas on one side (I was studying for a geography exam) and my notes on the other. I said to myself: 'Now, I really want to study well in order to do God's will, and I won't go ahead unless I know the material covered as well as I know the Hail Mary.' And this is what I did.

"I felt my studying was like incense offered to God because it was a matter of doing God's will well. I remember I had the impression that that last hour of study was a real masterpiece. When the hour was over, it was time to do another will of God: to prepare the meal for the Focolarine, who were coming back from work, since I was the only one at home.

"That day I was told to leave my studies permanently. I was happy because life is love; it is not study. What mattered was doing God's will, for that was the way to love.

"If we study in this way, there is no danger that we will become overly attached to our studies."

We also try to study in the right way because study "done well can favor contemplation." Teresa of Avila, doctor of the Church, was convinced of this, and she was an expert in contemplation. She felt that learned people, "if they are truly learned, are aided in contemplation," and therefore in acquiring wisdom.

The following words from 1960 tell us more about how to approach study.

"Studying has no value for us unless it is a fruit of our love. It has been said that 'the unlearned rise up and snatch the kingdom of God, and we, with all our study, are going to the depths of hell.' This was said about those who gave more importance to study than to the spirit of piety, of prayer."

WE STUDY BECAUSE WE LOVE

For us, then, love must be the reason for our study. I found the following text of mine:

"Why do we want to study? Why do we never want to stop studying?

"Because we love God. When you love someone, when you fall in love, you want to know everything about the other person.

"We want to know all we can about God so that we can love him more and more. In this way, studying will not be a burden for our soul, something that turns off our spirit of contemplation, but it will be like fuel added to the fire."

Moreover, study must not only be the effect of charity, but it must also serve charity.

For us, as for Saint Bernard, all knowledge, and the knowledge of scripture itself, must "serve charity." Bernard himself said in a famous sermon, "All my lofty philosophy, today, consists in knowing that Jesus *is*, and that he was crucified."

And when Bernard began to journey with his first companions along the path that God had indicated to him, and "he chose God alone," it is said that "his life with these companions was charity." "People who saw how they loved one another recognized that God was in them."

It must be the same for us, including those who dedicate much time to study.

Love must be the soul of study.

Speaking to a group of intellectuals, John Paul II said that scholars and theologians should keep Thérèse of Lisieux before them as their model because love is what can make a living theology.[8]

He might well have referred to Saint Thomas Aquinas as the model of scholars. Instead, the Pope pointed to Thérèse of Lisieux.

---

8. Talk to the Congregation for the Doctrine of the Faith, *L'Osservatore Romano*, 25 October 1997, p. 5.

A New Doctrine

We have long thought that the charism of unity or, better still, the life of unity would give rise to a doctrine. In fact, as the Father generated the Son, his Word, his Light, his Beauty, the life of unity will bring forth a theory, a doctrine.

Here are some thoughts about this:

"Without your life this doctrine could not come to be, just as the Father needs to exist in order to generate the Son, for the doctrine is like the Son in relation to the Father. This new reality (the doctrine), which involves us all, would not keep going if we were not living in this way. . ."

"This gospel-based life is like a school, indeed, like the source of a new doctrine that sums up and broadens the fields of knowledge already acquired."

"This doctrine will be a new synthesis, because the ideal of unity brings about the unity of opposites. In the theological field there are many schools: the ideal has the power, with Jesus in our midst, to bring about a synthesis and not a compromise."

And we see this doctrine as related to Mary:

"A new theology will emerge, a theology of the Church, which is also a Marian theology because it is the theology of the Work of Mary. The presence of Mary here, with her particular charism, will help us to gather all the fruits that have emerged down through the centuries from all the charisms, all the schools of thought, so as to bring about a new synthesis, a Marian synthesis, the synthesis which humanity awaits today. . . . And this will bathe the face of the Church not only with love but with light because Jesus is the light that came into the world."

One day, while I was speaking with an Apostolic Nuncio in Africa about the "seeds of the Word" present in every culture, I seemed to understand that the doctrine which comes from the charism of unity is not based on any human culture, for it comes from the Holy Spirit.

And thus this doctrine is a light that has no specific "color." It is a white light that can serve all cultures; it can pierce to the depths of each human being because Jesus is the man, not just *a* man but *the* Man.

I wrote this about the indigo:

"What I am interested in is the doctrine that is being drawn out. I don't drink wine by eating grapes. I drink wine after the grapes have been crushed. The wine refers to the doctrine drawn out from the bunch of grapes and the bunch of grapes refers to our entire experience. The wine is the doctrine with which we must all be inebriated: all illuminated, all happy."

THE ABBA SCHOOL

The following are rather new thoughts, which undoubtedly contain a prediction.

"Our impression is that the Lord is not only developing a new doctrine in the Work of Mary, but he is also incarnating it in the most varied forms of life, and these will form a whole range of fields of experimentation and will be, in themselves, part of the school (the 'inundations' are linked to the Abba School[9]).

---

9. The Abba School is an interdisciplinary group of scholars of the Focolare Movement who meet together to explore the doctrinal content of Chiara Lubich's charism.

"Consequently, in order to study Christian social doctrine competently (in view of our specific contribution), we will have to consider how people live in those industries and business firms that the Work of Mary will build. Likewise, to be thoroughly knowledgeable about the problems associated with education, we will have to examine the schools in which our ideal is lived. Thus, the entire Work of Mary will appear like a testing ground for this doctrine; and, at the same time, it will generate the doctrine."

What we have been saying since 1967 is noteworthy:

"I would like our Movement (given that the contribution we must give to the Church is not to be so much something like, for example, the *Compagnons Bâtisseurs*[10]) to be a work of light.

"Our spirituality should give rise to a culture, a philosophy, a sociology, a theology. It is something very much to be hoped for. What I mean is that among all the concrete things that should emerge from the Focolare Movement, this one is the most appropriate, the most logical.

"This would be one of the works, I believe, that our Movement must accomplish precisely because it has a spirituality.

"Since it is Christianity seen with the eye of the twentieth century, with the demands of the twentieth century, which presupposes all of the past, it must perforce have its scholars."

We find signs of our present-day Abba School already in 1974.

---

10. An association that began in Belgium in 1953 with the aim of helping the victims of the Second World War.

"Reading these pages[11] gave you glimmer of insight that made you understand a number of things. Above all, they gave you a surge of hope that these glimmers would one day become light. These glimmers of insight were of the most varied sort, going from the field of sociology to that of politics and of science. Now we have come together today, precisely to start gathering these insights.

"However, nothing of all this can come about unless we are able to re-create that climate, that atmosphere of unity, that most elevated unity which is the 'Soul.'[12] I think that today, 2 December 1974, could remain a historic day because it could mark the rebirth of the Work of Mary's doctrine."

Mary, Model of Wisdom

I would like to conclude with a thought taken from the Book of Wisdom:

Wisdom is radiant and unfading,
and she is easily discerned
by those who love her,
and is found by those who seek her.
She hastens to make herself known
to those who desire her.

---

11. The pages come from the years 1949 and 1950 and contain the intuitions referred to in the following footnote.
12. This expression of Chiara Lubich refers to an experience of profound unity experienced by her with the first men and women Focolarini in 1949 and then transmitted to the members of the Focolare. The notion of the "Soul" brings to mind the life of the first Christians, "The community of believers was of one heart and mind" (Acts 4:32).

> One who rises early to seek her
> will have no difficulty,
> for she will be found sitting at the gate.
> To fix one's thought on her
> is perfect understanding,
> and one who is vigilant on her account
> will soon be free from care.
> (Wis 6:12–15)

Our Lady is called the Seat of Wisdom, not because she spoke, not because she was a doctor of the Church, not because she had a professorial chair, not because she founded a university. She is the Seat of Wisdom because she gave Christ, Wisdom Incarnate, to the world. She did something concrete. It is the same for us: we shall have wisdom if we live in such a way that Jesus is in us, is among us, that his presence is concrete.

Love Unites

We will now take a look at the final "aspect" of the spirituality of unity, the one that concerns social communication and that we often refer to as the "violet."

Our Model

The model for the violet, as with all the other aspects, is in the life of the Most Holy Trinity, where there is perfect communication. We can understand this from what Jesus said, referring to the Father: "All I have is yours" (Jn 17:10).

I prepared what I am going to say by analyzing, as I did in other years, the documents from the Movement's past history (writings, talks, diaries, and so on), and I realized that the Statutes deal with this subject quite extensively. All that remains for me to do, then, is to gather some specific points and to offer them in order to keep us aware of our obligations, both great and small.

I decided to do this by relating what the Spirit has given us throughout these fifty-nine years of the Focolare's life, taking one decade at a time.

The '50s

I was reminded of the '50s when I received a long letter from Pope John Paul II, sent to me when, on 20 January 2000, the citizenship of Rome was conferred upon me. This letter gave me great joy because of its kind suggestions to me, among which the Pope wrote: "I call down upon you the strength and the light of the Holy Spirit, so that you may continue to be a courageous witness of faith and love, not only among the members of the Focolare, but also among all those you meet along your way."

This was something new, an unprecedented directive on the part of the Holy Father, which immediately turned my thoughts back to a writing from 1951, a page that continues to be fundamental.

At that time the Focolare Movement was not as it is now. It existed in an undeveloped form, with only the men and women Focolarini, some well-prepared lay people and youth, and a few men and women religious and diocesan priests. Probably because the consecrated people (that is, the men and women Focolarini) stood out among all the others, the whole Movement was called the "Order of Mary," following the example of other religious families. This writing was entitled: *How the Order of Mary relates those who do not belong to it*.[1]

It began like this:

"The Order of Mary does not live for itself.

"Like Mary, who lived only for Jesus, the Order of Mary lives for the Church. It lives, also for those who are not directly part of it and finds its (fulfillment, its) sanctity, in

---

1. Author's Note: I will quote from some early writings; many were originally spoken and later written down, and have been adapted to put them into written language.

loving them. By doing so, the Order of Mary lives out the law of the gospel, which requires us to die in order to live: 'Those who lose their life . . . will find it' (Mt 10:39).

"Wherever there is disunity, cold, worldliness, the cross, loneliness, illness, war, strife, and so on, the Focolarini, forgetting themselves, bring unity, warmth, heaven, company, health, peace, and harmony.

"Thus the Order of Mary is open to action in all fields: in families, schools, workplaces, government offices, convents of every spirituality, associations. It is open to kind of every human and religious society [we already foresaw, for example, a renewed politics and economy]."

"A fraternal relationship is established — because of the ideal of unity itself — between the Focolarini and other people [at this point we are only talking about the Catholic world]; and Jesus, who already lives among the Focolarini united in his name, will be able to live and does live also among us and others, drawing all to be one in God, in Love.

"Therefore, the only innovation that the Focolarini want to bring about is love, which they know is capable of changing the face of the earth. The only new organization is that of the Order of Mary, because everything is already organized in the Church. But the Focolarini want to contribute to the life of all the organizations so that everything that is done in the Church may be done in love, in a more profound and a more constant way, giving them new value. . . .

"They know that nothing is better organized than that which is put in order by love.

"The Focolarini love and admire all the different 'ways' that exist, because in all of them they find an aspect of the beauty of Jesus, who is *the* way, in which they would like everyone to walk, united in love, in order to break down the divisions, partitions, provincial attitudes, and all that is not catholic, that is, not universal."

That was the excerpt from 1951.

We know that with time other branches, like that of the priests, the Volunteers, the Gen 2, Gen 3, Gen 4, the men and women Religious, and so forth, came to be part of that Order of Mary, which then became the Work of Mary. But it becomes increasingly clear to us that they belong to it for the sake of the Church — as various instruments that foster the bond which the Movement must have with other realities present in the Church.

And already we have a glimpse of the unity developing between the Movement and the communities within the Church, both the modern and the ancient ones.

Considering the above writing, then, in the light of the Pope's guidance given on 22 January 2000, we cannot but see it as being remarkably relevant. It is a writing that expresses the soul of the violet, that is the drive to live outside ourselves, for others, the duty to communicate the treasure we possess.

Continuing in the '50s, we turn to a talk given to the people in charge of the zone which emphasizes that this "seventh aspect"[2] should be lived first of all within the Work of Mary, where it must nurture our mutual love:

"What belongs to one should be communicated to the others, at least to those around us, so that brotherly communion may grow.

_____

2. That is, the violet, since it is the seventh of the seven aspects of love, corresponding to the "last" color in the rainbow.

"To this end, we should always try to foster mutual love among the members of the Focolare through phone calls, letters, etc. It is normal practice for us to communicate in an appropriate way whatever we know; by doing so the Focolare continues to be a body in which the blood is always circulating."

Back in the '50s, one of the first ideas on the violet was about our magazine, which is an instrument of communication. It was seen as a way of conveying the spirit we wish to live by (it transmitted opinions, and so had a limited circulation) and was a means of keeping us united. In a letter of mine from March 1958, we read:

"We have learned that many people like our magazine because several articles convey the Ideal. Imagine what it would be like if the magazine were to reach fifty, seventy, even one hundred thousand people. Through the experiences printed there, which may relate small incidents but contain the essence of all cultures, that is, the gospel, Jesus could (bit by bit) set the world ablaze with his love and use the magazine as an instrument for keeping us all connected."

Reading this letter, we spontaneously thank God for the twenty-nine editions of the magazine, and for the seventy thousand copies printed in the Italian edition alone!

The '60s

We found appealing the fact that unity — as we noted from Jesus' prayer — cannot be disconnected from universality, because it says "May all be one." In one writing it says:

"If this Ideal had come on earth during the times of Saint Francis, for example, it would not have been achievable because America had not yet been discovered.

"In this century, instead, unity is possible. Since we were born in the era of airplanes, radio, and television, we are more likely to reach unity, always assuming that we are up to the task. And it will come about in a natural, unspectacular way — certainly not in our generation, and perhaps not even in the next or the one after that, but little by little it will, yes, all over the world."

Here is another thought from those years with regard to the universality of our ideal of unity:

"Jesus' Testament does not only say 'May they be one as you and I,' but it says 'May *all* be one.'

"Our focolares, our Movement would be a closed circle if we did not have universality as well as unity. If the stamp of universality does not go hand in hand with our unity, our unity is false.

"Our religious community is the world. We must, certainly, come together in community, gather with one another ('ecclesiastical' comes from *assembly*, *to gather together*), but . . . to gather together everyone."

During the '60s the thing that dominated our minds and our hearts was Mary Desolate at the foot of the cross, when Jesus entrusted to her a new maternity, as mother of John, in whom all people were represented. The Holy Spirit had been intent upon revealing Mary Desolate to us and making us love her, very deeply, under many different aspects: not just as a masterpiece of all virtues, but specifically as the universal mother, who with her love keeps all people together as her children. This is why we link the figure of Mary with the violet.

These were also the years in which we began to speak about the monthly reports sent to the Center of Movement as an instrument of the violet. I found a writing from Oberiberg, in Switzerland (where we used to spend the summer, even though we carried on working while we were there): "This is the year of the reports. It was precisely in her desolation that Mary became the bond of unity with all her children, because it was in her desolation that she paid for her universal spiritual maternity.

"We should relate our reports to Mary. While the reports may seem to be bureaucratic tools, in reality they are a way for Mary to stay in touch with us, in her Work [we always envisioned the Focolare as her Work] spread throughout the world."

With regard to the reports, we find written:

"The reports are somewhat like the Acts of the Apostles. In a hundred years, people will go to our archives to read our acts, acts of us early 'apostles' of the ideal of unity. For example, they will want to know how the Ideal was born and developed in France, what it brought to Algeria, and so on.

"They are the record of a Work of God. They demonstrate how Mary acted, how she governed, how she reigned in this Work.

"At times, certain Works are studied merely on the basis of historical documents. These documents are like the photograph of a Work, and they represent the living presence of a past that has determined the present."

The following reference to Paul is also revealing.

"Updating[3] is essential, just as is our outreach and everything else we do.

"I am reading the Acts of the Apostles. Wherever Paul goes, he sows widely and then he always leaves a small group of disciples. These he cultivates by visiting them again, by letters, by exhortations, by living with them for long periods of time, and by setting up among them the ecclesiastical hierarchy that will continue his work.

"When he returns to already established communities, he updates the disciples on all that the Lord has done through him, and they all give glory to God."

Our way of doing things follows the same line.

No aspect, however, not even the violet, has any value if it is not based upon that which is the very foundation of the Work of Mary: the presence of Jesus among us. The violet must always contribute toward supporting, nurturing, and recomposing this presence.

Meaningful in this regard is a page of my diary from the '60s in which we find the "norm of all norms," the "premise of every other rule." It speaks of the One who links people and makes them one.

We read: "Jesus among us is the soul of the 'violet.' Without him whatever means we use are dead and useless. . . .

"Wherever he is present, the Church is alive with the new face given to her by the Council.

"Everything is alive, alive, alive, because of his presence, which is linked to several aspects of unity: unity with those in authority, unity among ourselves, unity with all humanity, and it brings with it the fragrance of

---

3. This term is used to indicate the internal communication of news regarding the life of the Work of Mary.

that infallibility which the Council attributes to the People of God (cf. *Lumen Gentium* 12).

"With him therefore, we are on safe ground. . . .

"We have to bear this in mind, keep it in our thoughts and above all in our actions, as a fixed idea, as the first natural duty of a Focolarino.

"Everything else (including the 'violet') is in second place."

Hence, for instance, whenever any kind of "updating" arrives from the Center, do not listen to it until Jesus in your midst is in control, that is until there is charity among everyone.

We speak of correspondence, too, emphasizing its importance.

"One of the activities we still tend to neglect in the focolares is correspondence.

"Since our vocation is not directly concerned with, for example, caring for the sick, or caring for orphans, or caring for prisoners, but we are concerned, rather, with nurturing people and, at times, 'converting' them, correspondence is our 'surgical instrument' for achieving this goal."

In another diary entry we find:

"Our Rule emphasizes our need to use the most 'effective' and 'modern' means, and it says that this is because of the necessity of bringing our ideas to the 'greatest number of people in need of God.'

"Therefore, we must not let ourselves rest; we should plan to use not only printed materials but also the radio (which we already do), television (which we are starting to use), cinema and the theater. These are all means to be entrusted to the Heart of Jesus, so that, in his own time, he can make them develop to the full by giving us the necessary ideas, technology and economic means."

We are also beginning to feel the need to take full advantage of all that has been communicated. It is good advice to go back and meditate — a little at a time — on all that material so rich in wisdom.

Some thought from the '70s

In May 1970 we reiterated the importance of the archives, that collect and order our documents.

"We are sorting out the archives," we read in a diary. "There are very important documents — treasures of our Movement — which we have collected year after year, and which express, for example, the gradual and increasingly affirmative approval given us by the Church.

"It is an inestimable wealth for all the centuries to come. In reading certain records we have the impression of reading a magnificent novel; it's the story of a work of God."

Of great importance, too, is a collection of what I wrote and said about our Rule (that is, the Statutes).

In fact over the years as I wrote our twelve Statutes which, as the Movement grew little by little, became increasingly complete, I always experienced a special grace to present the Movement both for that time period and for the future, almost as if the charism contained a prophetic element.

A diary from 1971 describes how we strive to live unity in my focolare. I mention it here as an example because we can see the fruit that comes from having always communicated everything, in such a way as to become always more fully one:

"The *philadelphia* in my focolare is more than real. It is from this, after my personal union with Jesus, that I draw the strength to face the crosses that each day brings.

"Here each of us is concerned about the other, according to the need of each. Here we go from wisdom, communicated spontaneously, to the most practical tips on health, dress, the house, food, in a continual daily help for each other, with sacrifices that often go unmentioned.

"Here, in other words, we are convinced that we will never be judged, but loved, excused, helped. Here even the slightest betrayal is inconceivable. Here flows the blood of home, but a heavenly home."

The '80s and '90s

"We have the means: the publishing houses and a few Saint Clare Centers.[4] Everything is in its infancy, but that does not matter. What matters is that each aims at achieving the goal for which God brought it about.

"We have our musical groups too, and these are a prelude to some form of theatre — and that will come! But, we repeat once again, most important of all is having Jesus in our midst.

"All our methods and means can be useful if we who use them are leaven, if we are salt."

With regard to the way to communicate the light of our ideal, we find:

---

4. That is the name given to the audio-visual centers of the Work of Mary and refers to Clare of Assisi, whom Pius XII proclaimed the patron of communication.

"We must be like reservoirs or dams, but these should not be opened up all at once. The water level must always remain high. We draw it from the life of the 'Ideal' that we lead, from the Holy Spirit within us, from the liturgy, from theology, from sacred history, from the Gospel. . . . But, I repeat, we must not open up the dam all at once. There are moments for doing this, for example, during the meetings of the Movement. So if I have a good idea or an intuition, I take note of it . . . and the water rises. . . . And then when there is a meeting, I pour a bit of water; then in another meeting I pour a bit more water, and in the same way also in my personal contacts."

This reference to the letters that circulated during the early days is beautiful and important: "These little letters (as we called them) are the most numerous documents that have remained from the early days. We wrote to our friends in order to draw them into our same ideal of life, to our parents and other relatives, and through them we wanted to reach many, many others. We wrote to married people, to priests (and we were just young girls), to religious. . . . And, just as fire envelops all that it meets along its way, just as nothing and no one escapes since its flames consume everything, so does a spiritual fire burn in those letters."

We also thought of the future of the Focolare. In 1984 I wrote:

"The years are passing and we must all understand that the hour that arrived for Pina[5] will come for us too, and maybe soon. I think of this, too, of course. But

---

5. Pina de Vettori, a Focolarina from the early times of the Movement, who had left for heaven during those days.

when I read all the material we have, or listen again to the tapes, or look over some of the papers. . . . I think that even a tiny piece of what I receive from them 'to live' would be enough to allow Jesus to live in me. The archives, properly used, make sure that everyone, anywhere in our Movement, knows how to live. And when I am no longer here, people will have to go back and listen again to what was said, and they will see that all these ideas, all these thoughts have the same value. Whether they appear big or small, they are all expressions of the charism. People will be able to start over from the beginning, because our spiritual journey had not been an ascent. Rather, we have penetrated more and more deeply into the Gospel, and the Gospel is always at the same level — it is always high, it is always 'Jesus.' They will start again from the beginning and they will see that the first word has the same value as the last. This is the reality."

In the '90s, in view of the programs on television that were often harmful and extremely negative, we gave some guidance on how to use it:

"We must be very prudent with the communications media. Indeed, we need to make a courageous, radical choice, which perhaps not everyone will understand: giving up, in a sense, television. We should only watch the news, religious, sports, cultural or nature programs, or well-made films that contain real values."

Once they had received this guidance from me, the response of the Focolarini was very positive; indeed, we can say that they were enthusiastic. "Giving up" television increased the supernatural atmosphere in the focolare, and its unity.

Of course, our circumstances in the Movement vary greatly, according to the duties of each person, but prudence is required of everyone.

In those years we saw the Holy Spirit as the protector of the means of communication:

"The Holy Spirit, whose task is to unite, cannot but be the patron of each means of communication."

We understood that the hour had come to preach our ideal "from the rooftops." "Until now we have gone rather gently, but no longer; we need to go out into public life, to speak out, to preach from the rooftops. As a consequence we must use the spoken word, but also newspapers and magazines, a wider circulation of the Word of Life,[6] books, printed matter in general, radio, television, documentaries . . . every means."

"Let's ask ourselves at the end of every day: did I speak more today than yesterday? This includes writing, or speaking among ourselves in order to keep the spiritual temperature high wherever we are and in the meetings we hold, etc. Speak, speak to others, seeking out every opportunity."

We also specified (when in the '90s the Pope had given some suggestions on the "new evangelization") that our evangelization consists in this: in living and in speaking.

The Pope said: "The Church's vocation to evangelization means above all living the Gospel more deeply. Such a witness lived every day is an initial act of

_____

6. The commentary (by Chiara Lubich herself) on a sentence of the scripture, which is lived monthly in the Focolare. It is translated into eighty-four languages and reaches fourteen million people throughout the world.

evangelization. But Christian witness through personal example also needs to be accompanied by the proclamation of Jesus Christ."[7]

This clarification of my own is also from the '90s: "The first instrument of unity is the source of the charism. Hence: unity with the source. This goes without saying. If God used a particular instrument to bring this charism to the earth, it is necessary to be united to it, which means taking all the water that this source gives and has given. For this reason too the archives are of enormous importance."

In recent years, the Saint Clare Center has been restoring the early tapes made back in the '60s, our early videos, which were becoming demagnetized. In doing so, they discovered such beautiful and important things that now many want copies of them.

We also try to document all that is the fruit of our Ideal life, archiving writings, magazines, audiovisuals, etc., in order to hand over to the future generations (to the Gen 2, Gen 3, and Gen 4) a legacy that will help them continue our revolution of love.

We understand the good that the means of communication can bring about:

"God must become fashionable again — it's a motto of ours — and he can come back into homes and every environment through television, theatre, newspapers, magazines, books, and interviews."

Lately it has become clear to us that we need to use the means of communication outside the Focolare Movement (as we already use them quite extensively

---

7. John Paul II, To the Bishops of Ghana, 6 November 1987, in *La Traccia* 11 (1987), pp. 122–125.

within it), ever since we were authoritatively told that our Movement (especially in its more "incarnated" aspects, like the "inundations") needs greater visibility.

We have accepted this suggestion for greater visibility while thinking of Jesus' words: "In the same way, let your light shine before others, so that they may see your good works and give glory to your Father in heaven" (Mt 5:16).

A new talk, rich in content and methodology, which does not appear, of course, in the Statutes, is the one addressed to the Congress on the Media held in June 2000. It would be good to read it again.

To conclude, I will mention at least one thought contained in this talk.

Jesus Forsaken, having made himself emptiness, infinite nothingness, is the pupil of the eye of God looking onto the world, and the pupil of the world looking onto God. Jesus Forsaken was therefore the most sublime, the most divine communicator. He joined heaven to earth and the earth to heaven.

He is the model for us who want to live this seventh aspect of our spirituality to the fullest.

Also Available from New City Press

A CALL TO LOVE
Spiritual Writings, vol. 1
by Chiara Lubich

"Chiara Lubich has established herself as a Christian writer of considerable proportions. Given her prolific literary output it is fitting that New City Press should issue a retrospective series of Lubich's best works, titled Spiritual Writings. The first work in this series *A Call to Love* comprises three of her most popular studies of momentous Christian living: *Our Yes to God* (1980), *The Word of Life* (1974), and *The Eucharist* (1977)."

B.C. Catholic

ISBN 1-56548-077-5, 2d printing, 5 1/8 x 8, 180 pp.

WHEN OUR LOVE IS CHARITY
Spiritual Writings, vol. 2
by Chiara Lubich

"The author draws on some of the best elements of the Catholic tradition to speak a credible word for the world today. The text actually is a compilation of three independent works with the first being the book's title. The other two sections are *Jesus in Our Midst* and *When Did We See You Lord?*"

The Cord

ISBN 0-911782-93-1, 2d printing, paper, 5 1/8 x 8, 152 pp.

CHRISTIAN LIVING TODAY
Meditations
by Chiara Lubich

"Like shafts of sunlight that break through the clouds on a dreary day, these meditations touch us and turn our most mundane activities into brightly lit God-moments."

Liguorian

ISBN 1-56548 -094-5, 7th printing, paper 5 1/8 x 8, 158 pp.

HEAVEN ON EARTH
Meditations and Reflections
by Chiara Lubich

Heaven on Earth is an inspiring collection of reflections spanning the past fifty years of Chiara Lubich's writing. This beautiful medley of meditations, all newly translated and many available for the first time in English, provides a striking, panoramic view of her gospel-based spirituality, centered around Jesus' last testament, "Father, may they all be one" (Jn 17:21).

"In these pages we are invited to drink from the spiritual sources which have nourished her own life and the lives of millions of others."

Michael Downey

ISBN 1-56548-144-5, paper, 5 1/8 x 8, 176 pp.

HERE AND NOW
Meditations on Living in the Present
by Chiara Lubich

Thought-provoking reflections to help us grasp and shape the "here and now" as God's gift to us.

Like footprints washed away in the sand, the past is gone; as for the future, it does not yet exist. In this series of inspiring meditations, Chiara Lubich shows us that living in the present is our way to be connected with what is unlimited: eternity. "Everything is in God's hands," she says, "He will allow only his will to be accomplished, and this is always for our good." Living the present moment puts us in touch, already here on earth, with heaven.

ISBN 1-56548-232-8, paper, 4 1/2 x 7, 72 pp.

JESUS: THE HEART OF HIS MESSAGE
Unity and Jesus Forsaken
by Chiara Lubich

"Without being simplistic or reductionistic, Lubich challenges her associates to focus on Jesus forsaken as the model for unity and the key to living a life of joy."

Bishop Robert Morneau

ISBN 1-56548-090-2, 2d printing, paper, 5 1/8 x 8, 112 pp.

MAY THEY ALL BE ONE
by Chiara Lubich

The author tells her story and that of the Focolare Movement. The perfect book for those who wish to know more about the Focolare and the spirituality of unity.

ISBN 0-911782-46-X, 7th printing, paper, 4 1/2 x 7, 92 pp.

JOURNEY TO HEAVEN
Spiritual Thoughts to Live
by Chiara Lubich

This is the third volume of Chiara's spiritual thoughts given in monthly conference calls. It is not only inspirational but it is a practical reference guide on how to live heavenly realities in our everyday lives.

ISBN 1-56548-093-7, paper, 5 1/8 x 8, 146 pp.

A LIFE FOR UNITY
An Interview with Chiara Lubich
by Franca Zambonini

"This little book's 175 pages of text are a fast and intriguing read. The insights are uplifting and Chiara's delight in a gospel that is still new and fresh after 2,000 years is contagious. She confirms that Christians are still known by their love for one another."

Catholic Advocate

ISBN 0-904287-45-9, 2d printing, paper, 5 1/8 x 8, 181 pp.